Promises
to Keep...

Garnett M. Wilder

HERITAGE BOOKS
2026

HERITAGE BOOKS

AN IMPRINT OF HERITAGE BOOKS, INC.

Books, CDs, and more—Worldwide

For our listing of thousands of titles see our website
at
www.HeritageBooks.com

A Facsimile Reprint
Published 2026 by
HERITAGE BOOKS, INC.
Publishing Division
5810 Ruatan Street
Berwyn Heights, MD 20740

International Standard Book Number
Paperbound: 978-0-7884-5169-0

DEDICATED

To Marian - *Ultima*

CONTENTS

INTRODUCTION

In offering this collection of sermons to a general readership I have somewhat the same question as that of Ezekiel as he viewed the valley of the dry bones: can these bones live again? They did live *once* for they were preached to a real congregation, and their flesh was the flesh of real people. Their tears, hopes, dreams, burdens and needs were the *viscera* of life. The reality of the sermon was an event, not an essay. The event *happened* in one or a thousand ways, in that collocation of preacher's intent, responder's perception, and God's Word which emerged.

In a sense, these offerings were never a sermon. They are the prepared text from which a sermon *happened*. As such, they are truly the bones around which flesh gathered and into which life was *breathed*. As *event* the sermon can never happen again. As Word of God, it was never more than a *possibility*. Nevertheless, a *new event* can take place -- in each reader. Word of God can be spoken to you.

Therefore, these messages are offered to the general reader in the same spirit and with the same hope that they were offered in the congregation. They come to you as from the *future*, as God's possibility for your life. Is there something God wants to say to you? I imagine so, for somehow this book came into your hands. Because of the nature of the sermon as an event which happens to you; because it is something you must interpret; because it is something about which you must decide; your life can be changed as a result of this encounter. In that case, God will have used the moment for his purpose. If so, the temerity of offering this bag of bones will have its own justification.

A certain contextual progression may be observed in the compilation of these messages. They are fewer than half the sermons preached during the course of my first year in a new pastorate. They form the nucleus of the preacher's intent with the congregation.

The first section, BEGINNING, is addressed to the identity of preacher and congregation, the purpose that compels us, the power that sustains us, the standard that guides us and the goal that attracts us.

The second section, BELIEVING, is addressed to those realities, experiences and understandings which make us what we are as persons of faith, as a community of believers for whom doubt is not a bad word and for whom worship, growth, and servanthood make sense.

The third section, DOING, is addressed to the conclusions which may be drawn from an understanding of who we are. It has something to do with the deepest needs we feel, the logical consequences of what we believe and the agenda which emerges. Since I have been known all my ministry as somewhat of an activist, the reader will please be reminded that no builder uses all his steel in the foundation.

A suggestion to the reader: read and meditate on the larger scriptural context; reflect on the meaning *for you* and for your personal situation what any of these words or allusions may mean; and ask God to say to you what he wants you to receive.

1

PROMISES TO KEEP

And taking the twelve again, he began to tell them what was to happen to him, saying, "Behold, we are going up to Jerusalem; and the Son of man will be delivered to the chief priests and the scribes, and they will condemn him to death, and deliver him to the Gentiles; and they will mock him, and spit upon him, and scourge him, and kill him; and after three days he will arise."   Mark 10:32b-34

The use of this particular scripture may seem strange to you. A new pastor is not like a lamb led to the slaughter nor a messianic figure moving toward a cross. But he or she is a person of destiny, or else he or she ought not to be there. Whether this is an appropriate scripture for beginning a new pastorate depends upon one's point of view. But this scripture certainly speaks to me today.

Jesus had gone up to Jerusalem many times for religious occasions. But *this time* going up to Jerusalem was an *event*, not just an occasion. It was qualitative time, not just quantitative time. It was destiny, not just duty. Jesus' sense of what might happen in Jerusalem may have had an ominous aspect, but it also had a tremendously optimistic quality. He may have anguished over the prospect of the cross he would bear. But make no mistake, he *wanted* to go to Jerusalem!

Jerusalem was where the action was. Jerusalem was where his witness would be the greatest. Jerusalem was where his destiny would take form and substance. So far as Jesus was concerned, as Jerusalem went, so went the world. Standing before Pontius Pilate he put his mission succinctly: "This is why I am in the world, that I might bear witness to the truth."

In my understanding every Christian attempts to identify with Jesus without developing a messianic complex. We are not the world-savers. But we are witnesses. In varying degrees we may have a sense of destiny — a sense that God is walking with us and that his purpose is being worked out in our lives. The feeling that God wants me in this pulpit at this point in time is almost overwhelming. I feel that I have been being prepared all my life for this place. This is where my witness will be made. This is where our destiny will take form and substance.

I remember returning home late in the evening a few years ago to the shocking news that my beloved teacher, Carl Michalson, had been killed in an airplane crash. Michalson was a world-famous theologian. The shock was great not merely because the news was so sudden but because I sensed that the world was cheated. He had so much to give. He was so young. He was only fifty years old! I later learned that Michalson had commented to his wife, "Janet, it appears that we have accomplished everything we set out to do. You have your art. I have written my books." Well, I do not have any premonitions that life is over. I have a tremendous anticipation that it is just beginning!

In my youth I made some promises to God. In a moment of surrender which has been repeated many times, I promised the Lord that I would be completely his. I promised that I would be faithful to witness to the best insights he would give to me. I promised that I would give him one hundred percent of my effort. Although I have fallen short almost constantly in the fulfillment of those vows, the promises are still very much a part of my consciousness. Now I make the same vow to you: I will be yours. I will be faithful to the task. And I will give it one hundred percent.

That poses problems. Merely to *suggest* a total effort creates skeptics -- and rightly so. We rarely live up to our own expectations, much less the expectations of others. Such a suggestion also creates anxiety. Some people don't want to deal with a total effort. It can appear impatient and even obnoxious.

I once saw an example of what total dedication would look like -- and it *did* appear impatient and obnoxious! I was living in New York State at the time and this man was being interviewed on one of the New York television stations. It would almost make one nervous to watch him.
He was energetic to the point of being frenetic.
He was opinionated to the point of arrogance.
He was self-possessed to the point of being
obnoxious.

I later learned that he was a doctor, a fact which explained a great deal! Doctors *have* to be energetic, opinionated, and self-possessed if they are going to be effective at their work. Translate that strong, competent, and confident. We want a leader to be strong, competent, and confident but we do not want him or her to be impatient, opinionated, and self-possessed!

The man I saw interviewed was Dr. Tom Dooley. He was not just self-possessed, he was *possessed*. He was possessed of a passion to help the people of southeast Asia in 1954-55. He had been deeply impressed with the utter misery he saw in that impoverished part of the world. He returned to the tiny kingdom of Laos as a civilian and set

up a hospital and clinic in the village of Muong Sing, just
five miles from the Red China border. Muong Sing is a
typical Asian village of about four thousand persons, nes-
tled in a twenty-five mile wide valley that had a scattered
population of about three million and, by American standards, only two doctors.

The story of Dooley's work in that area has been told
all over the world. He is now a famous symbol of humanitarian service and Christian witness. His organization, Medico, channels the generosity of doctors, nurses,
pharmaceutical companies, and other companies and individuals to humanitarian projects in many areas of desperate need.

Those of you who know the story of Dooley's work
were surely impressed by his almost frantically intense
use of time. He worked night and day ministering to immediate needs, training others, and telling the story to
the world. Dooley's compulsive concern for his use of
time may have been a premonition. He developed cancer
and died while still a very young man. He did not curse
his fate. He did his work with the time that he had.

Perhaps the power of Dooley's witness is focused in
the words of Robert Frost engraved on the back of the St.
Christopher medal which he wore:
> The woods are lovely, dark, and deep.
> But I have promises to keep,
> And miles to go before I sleep.

Those words speak for me, too. The life of Decatur
First United Methodist is long and distinguished. You and
I did not start it nor are we likely to end it. We may be
lulled into the assumption that we are only an individual
interlude in its distinguished history. On the contrary,
Decatur First is Jerusalem for each one of us. This is
where the action is. This is where our destiny takes form

and substance. So far as we are concerned, as Decatur goes, so goes the world! This is where we can make our greatest witness.

I trust that I have not been speaking primarily of myself today. The fact is that each of us has made a promise to God. It is also true that our time is running out. How much time do we have? An hour? A day? A year? Ten years? Today is an appropriate time for each of us to reassess our promises and to take note of the hour. We have promises to keep, and miles to go before we sleep.

2

IS SURVIVAL ENOUGH?

*You are the salt of the earth; but if salt
has lost its taste, how shall its saltness be
restored? It is no longer good for anything
except to be thrown out and trodden under foot
by men.*

Matthew 5:13

This has been a great fourth of July weekend! Laziness, sunburn, the Peachtree Road Race, mobs of people,
a Braves win, fabulous fireworks -- and solemn thoughts
about the condition of our country. Jack Anderson, probably our most infamous muckraking reporter, observed
that we have been rocked by one news shock after another
until our confidence in America has been shaken:

> Fifty-three of our countrymen in humiliating
> bondage. Greedy oil shiekdoms...reducing
> us to supplicant status, the Russians defying
> us in Cuba and Afghanistan...a recession at
> home...riots in Miami....dismaying evi-
> dence that political corruption didn't end with
> Watergate.

In spite of it all Anderson concludes that the United
States is still the best country in the world, the land of

dreams for oppressed people everywhere. This is how he says it:

> I feel in my gut that this wracked land still of-
> fers the best and brightest hope for the future.
> In 1814, the British redcoats seized Washing-
> ton and burned the White House and we survived.
> Before the Civil War, we lived half slave and
> half free and we survived. Time and again,
> depressions gripped the land and we survived.
> In the 1940's, the Hitler holocaust threatened
> the world, and we helped the world survive.
>
> (Atlanta Constitution, July 4, 1980)

It seems significant to me that Anderson should feel such a need to reassure us. We *are* in a state of shock! Our confident self-image is severely threatened. The most poignant note in Anderson's commentary is that of survival. We are in a survival mentality in this country -- and that can be bad! A survival mentality almost always is accompanied by the erosion of values. This is a good time to ask whether survival is enough.

Marian and I began our ministry together after World War II when we had just come through another period of the survival mentality. Our treatment of Japanese Ameri-cans and other incidents during that period indicate that we do not perform well in such a state of mind. It is easy to become cynical at those times. One day an elderly minister's wife said to Marian, "Methodist people are the worst people in the world." I did not believe it then and I do not believe it now. On the contrary, Methodist people are the *best* people in the world! Jesus expressed it pointedly to those who were gathered around him. He said, "You are the salt of the earth." He did not need to elaborate. Those people knew that salt was the crucial ingredient of their lives. It's saving, preserving, healing, and vitalizing qualities were well known. In American history the Christian people have indeed been the salt of the society.

But with this accolade Jesus gave a warning: "But if the salt has lost its savor, it is thenceforth good for nothing but to be thrown out." He said in effect, "Don't lose it!" As we celebrate this Independence Day, it does not seem too much to suggest that this advice of our Lord is appropriate for us. What is it in our heritage that is *worth* saving? We are certainly in a survival mentality in our country. But is survival *enough?*

Survival has always been elemental for nature's creatures, humans included. Perhaps survival has been *ultimate.* We are tempted to make it so today. But in the last hundred years survival has been raised to the level of a science, both in terms of technology and theory. The publication of Charles Darwin's *Origin of the Species* stimulated a movement of ideas which has had a tremendous effect upon the world of science and philosophy and religion. The resulting debate did not do credit to either science or religion. In the long run religion appeared to get the worst of it. This was not because men and women of religion did not finally come to terms with Darwin's theories, but because they insisted upon staking the whole truth of God upon a traditional idea of how the world came into being.

The primary thesis which was so heatedly discussed was called *the survival of the fittest.* This hypothesis was that a process of mutation takes place in the development of animal life by which certain animal forms are better adapted to survive in the struggle of the natural world. An animal type may add, over a vastly extended period of time, some new feature which gives it an advantage over others of its type in a given environment. The more advanced type survives while the less advanced type becomes extinct. In this way, according to Darwin, new animal forms are developed. A few years later Darwin extended this theory to suggest that man and the ape-type animals were evolved from a common ancestor. The idea

of the survival of the fittest has had a profound influence
upon our thinking and our way of life.

Close onto Darwin's publication of his theories the
philosopher Friedrich Nietzsche suggested that the purpose of the human race was to carry through this devel-
opmental process to the highest level. This new being,
the superman, will be a combination of the genius and the
saint, including both strength and compassion. Nietzsche
propounded the idea of *the survival of the strong*. For
him, the strong are destined to master the weak. Somewhere along the way, Nietzsche's dream became a nightmare.

We have lived through the philosophy of the survival
of the fittest and then the philosophy of the survival of the
strong. These have been disastrous. Now we are tempted to live by the philosophy of *the survival of the shrewd*.
Political regimes all over the world, whether they be
Communist or otherwise, have demonstrated that they
will use whatever methods are necessary to maintain
power. When survival of vested interests is at stake,
the end always justifies the means.

There *must* be some people in the world to challenge
this trend! We must be those people!

One of the most sobering lessons of history is the
development of Nazi Germany. The Nazis took advantage
of a people who had contributed the very best to European
culture. German science, theology, music, and philosophy have had a profound impact on Western culture. After
World War I Germany was defeated, humiliated. In the
midst of this bitterness and disillusionment a man shouted, "Germany will recover. We shall recover our lost
pride. We shall recover our lost possessions. We shall
rule the world!"

Students of history know only too well how alarmingly close to success Adolph Hitler came. But the price
was astounding. In the name of recovery Germany submitted to a beastly morality -- a brutal tyranny. She sold
her soul. This involved practically everybody, including
some of the most prominent theologians of the German
Church. On the basis of the doctrine of the separation of
church and state (more precisely, "the powers that be
are ordained of God") they developed a religious ground
for the nonconcern of the Church with political developments.

These "political developments" included the abolition
of democratic government, the establishment of brothels
for the German army, experimental programs of human
breeding and the annihilation of twelve million people!

To be sure, there were voices of protest within the
Church. But these voices were soon silenced by execu-
tion or imprisonment. In the name of recovery Germany
submitted to the philosophy of the survival of the strong.
One of those imprisoned, Martin Niemoeller, said:

> In Germany they came first for the Commu-
> nists, and I didn't speak up because I wasn't
> a Communist. Then they came for the Jews,
> and I didn't speak up because I wasn't a Jew.
> Then they came for the trade unionists, and
> I didn't speak up because I wasn't a trade
> unionist. Then they came for the Catholics,
> and I didn't speak up because I was a Protes-
> tant. Then they came for me, and by that
> time no one was left to speak up.

After the war, film reports were made of the concentration camps. These recounted atrocities so vast that
our minds were hardly able to assimilate the scope of
their horror. We saw, but some of us only dimly com-
prehended, the extent of what can become the order of the

day when "law and order" are allowed to stand as a substitute for justice.

Later, a drama was presented on television titled
Trial at Nuremburg. This drama was a documentary based
upon the trial of a group of German war criminals. These
were not ordinary criminal types. They were not blood-
thirsty sadists. They were the justices of the German
High Court! The charge against them was that they had
established the legal precedents for dealing with what was
then called "the Jewish problem." It was they who legiti-
mized the elimination of Jews from German society.

The defense of these men was a masterpiece of rationalization. It was claimed that what they did was the
highest form of patriotism. By remaining flexible in the
face of Hitler's demands they had preserved the structure
of legality for the German people. Further, their guilt
was no worse than that of the British and the Americans
who early approved Hitler and sold war goods to him.
Yes, if they were guilty then all were guilty. Thus, no
one is guilty!

Toward the end of the trial more subtle private pressures were applied. It was suggested to the American
Chief Judge that to condemn these men would be an affront
to the German people who were by this time our allies
against the Russians.

Nevertheless, the American judge condemned the
atrocities and convicted the defendants. Later in the
judge's chambers he was confronted by his military atta-
ché who said, "Sir, you have made a decision we will find
very difficult to live with over here. Don't you understand
that we are in a struggle for survival?" The American
judge replied, "It is not enough to survive!"

The judgment at Nuremburg was not merely a judgment of a small group of men nor even a judgment of one nation. It was a judgment of civilization. It is obvious that we are today in a struggle for survival. There is also no question in my mind but that we must remain as strong as possible, as fit as possible, and as shrewd as possible. But we *must not* capitulate to the philosophy of the survival of the strong or the survival of the shrewd!

In the Nuremburg drama the American judge was asked to talk with the German Chief Justice, who tried to convince him that his motives were honorable. Finally the German judge said, "I did not know it would go that far." The American replied, "It went that far the first time you condemned a man you knew to be innocent."

Someone has suggested that what happens in human affairs usually depends on who is allowed to set the pace which others follow. You and I must be the pacesetters in our society. As Saint Paul said, "We who are strong have a responsibility to those who are weak." (Romans 15:1) You are the salt of the earth! Your saving, healing, preserving, and vitalizing qualities are essential to the making of a better world.

In one of Petrarch's *Letters of Old Age* we find this admonition:

> When a word must be spoken to further a good
>   cause,
> and those whom it behooves to speak remain
>   silent,
> anybody ought to raise his voice,
> and break a silence which may be frought with
>   evil...

> Many a time a few simple words have helped
> further the welfare of a nation, no matter who
> uttered them; the voice itself displaying its
> latent powers sufficed to move the hearts of men.

24

3

THINGS THAT WON'T WAIT

Therefore, having this ministry by the mercy of God, we do not lose heart. We have renounced disgraceful, underhanded ways; we refuse to practice cunning or to tamper with God's word, but by the open statement of the truth we would commend ourselves to every man's conscience in the sight of God.

II Corinthians 4:1,2

Lyle Shaller is one of the foremost analysts of Protestant churches in this country. His basic premise for church planning is: "If you don't know where you are going, any road will take you there." We are accustomed to setting goals in most aspects of our church planning. Yet we seldom set an overall goal for our congregational life. Saint Paul set a goal for the church at Corinth. He said:

Now the Lord is the Spirit, and where the Spirit of the Lord is, there is freedom. And we all, with unveiled face, beholding the glory of the Lord, are being changed into his likeness from one degree of glory to another, for this comes from the Lord who is the Spirit.

(II Corinthians 3:17, 18)

This is the God-given goal for any congregation: that we each, by degrees and in our own separate ways, are increasingly becoming more like Christ. It is my job as your pastor and preacher to lead you individually and collectively in that development.

For us to have a clear perception of our goal and the place of our various ministers in the growth process is essential. Many churches, having no clearly focused concept of their goal, seem content for congregation and clergy to ride off in all directions, every individual or group merely "doing their own thing." In his letter to Corinth Paul concentrates on his own personal relationship to the congregation. I want to take the liberty to do that today.

How can I be the most effective pastor to you? My own experience has taught me that I have been the most effective pastor when, over a period of years, simply walking with persons in caring concern through the dark valleys of pain, grief, and trouble produced a loving bond of Christian friendship. If, as the saying goes, "It takes a lot o' livin' to make a house a home," then it surely takes a lot of living with his/her people to make a person a good pastor.

To become an effective *preacher* requires a good deal more than that. The preacher is effective when the Spirit of God uses him/her to stimulate the minds and hearts of persons. The relationship with God is primary, but the relationship with people is also essential. The preacher lives constantly in the tension of those two relationships. The temptation and the tendency is to let these aspects get out of proportion.

The conventional wisdom expresses it this way: "You have to earn the right to speak." Translated, that means: Don't speak out on anything controversial until the people love you enough to allow you to get by with it. Of course, there is a great deal of truth in that conventional wisdom. It is the sort of pragmatic truth which is so alluring, especially to Americans. We normally respond better to preachers whom we like.

However, there is also an element of falsehood in the conventional wisdom. *God's* truth is that we do not become preachers by popular mandate nor merely because we think we might like the job. St. Paul says, "We have this ministry by the mercy of God." We are *called* to it. A sense of necessity prompts us to the task. To remain faithful to the Lord as a preacher involves overcoming monumental temptations. Paul mentions them. He says, "We have renounced underhanded ways; we refuse to practice cunning or to tamper with God's word." Do you realize how much leverage a preacher gives up when he/she: 1. renounces underhanded (manipulative) ways; 2. refuses to try to outwit or outmaneuver people; or 3. refuses to use God's word to reinforce his/her own opinions and prejudices?

Paul wants his relationship with the people at Corinth to be aboveboard. He says, "By the open statement of the truth we would commend ourselves to every person's conscience in the sight of God." I think this gives clear guidance as to how the preacher may be more effective. He/she comes as one called of God to the task, who speaks as straightforwardly as possible, and who trusts the rest of it to each individual conscience under the guidance of God.

This idea challenges the conventional wisdom. What this says is that the mandate of the preacher comes from God, not the people. The responsibility is to speak the truth as clearly as one can ascertain it. There are some things which in the nature of the case will not wait for some indeterminate rapport-time in the future. What are these things which won't wait?

First of all, *truthfulness won't wait.* There is a subtle seductiveness to the desire to be accepted. We know historically as well as instinctively that the bearer of bad tidings is not as well received as the bearer of glad tidings. Consequently, there is a tendency on the part of the preacher to share only *half* the tidings -- the good part! If perchance the preacher dares to address the issues of the day by the claims of God's righteousness, there is still the tendency to address only those matters which the congregation deems acceptable. For example, such a preacher would go easy on gambling in Las Vegas and the dangers of tobacco smoking in North Carolina!

Saint Paul refused that ticket -- and so do I. You deserve better than that. You deserve -- and God requires -- that I give you the fullest and best truth I know. Harold Bosley tells of the Old Testament scholar a few years ago who was publishing a radical theory on the authorship of Isaiah. He admitted that he shrank from the hail of criticism he was sure to receive. But he said, "There is a worse fate than being misunderstood; it is to be to truth a timid friend."

Second, *authority won't wait.* If the preached word is no more than a matter of opinion, no matter how well-informed, then disagreement ends the process. One opinion may be regarded equally as good as the other. The Roman Catholics address this problem by the idea of the final authority of the Pope and the fundamentalists do it with a simplistic literalism. We Methodists have neither of those. This is all the more reason why we should have a clear understanding of what is happening to us in a sermon.

What would *you* accept as authoritative? The answer to that question may vary as widely as the number of people here today. Age differences, cultural differences, peer group differences, and personal experiences all contribute to our perception of what is truth for us. For example, if you were talking to your child about how he or she ought to live, would you

    1. reason with him/her?
    2. point out the dangers?
    3. or use scriptural values?

Of course, we would probably use all three in varying degrees. But even the extent of our emphasis on one or the other would reflect an assumption about what would carry the most weight in a given instance.

The marvelous thing to me about preaching is that God takes the limited understanding and perception of the preacher, adds it to the myriad understandings and perceptions of the congregation and *speaks his Word* to each one! It may be a different word according to your needs. But it will be God's Word to you. I think this is what Paul means when he says, "We have this treasure in earthen vessels, to show that the transcendent power belongs to God and not to us." (II Corinthians 4:7) In a limited vessel and to limited vessels God brings his Word!

A sermon is not a speech or a proclamation. It is an *event*. The sermon only *begins* with the preacher. It is completed in the heart of each individual listener and in the body of the whole congregation. When preached word is transformed into Word of God for you, it will carry its own authority to the degree that you recognize it as God's claim on your life.

Finally, *events won't wait*. When our niece was only four years old she was sitting one day in the room with her mother. She broke the silence with a deep sigh, and exclaimed, "Oh, the vicissitudes of life!" I suppose that even four year olds have discovered that events do not arrive on our schedule.

Wouldn't it be wonderful if we as Christians could be fully prepared to answer the questions which come at us from all sides and in the most difficult of circumstances? I saw a sermon topic one time which intrigued me. It read, "When Life Tumbles in — What Then?" I always wanted to know what the preacher said. On those occasions when life has tumbled in on me, I have never been quite ready. Sometimes, the more I struggle with a question, the more complex it becomes. There is hardly a social problem which does not boggle the mind in its complexity.

The best we can do with domestic problems is to try to deal with them in the strength and guidance of the Lord. We may not have an answer to social problems, whether national or international. Nevertheless, there *is* something we can do.

We can become better informed.

We can create a climate of searching for answers within the Christian community.

We can refuse to retreat into conclaves of criticism.

We can offer support to our leaders rather than recalcitrant resistance.

We can live in the light of the Christian awareness that God is moving with us through the agonizing struggles of life. That awareness changes the tone of everything, so that with Saint Paul we can say:

We are afflicted in every way, but not crushed;
perplexed, but not driven to despair; persecuted,
but not forsaken; struck down, but not destroyed;
always carrying in the body the death of Jesus,
so that the life of Jesus may be manifested in
our bodies.   (II Corinthians 4:8-10)

4

POWER FAILURE

*I know that you have but little power, and
yet you have kept my word and have not denied
my name.* Revelation 3:8
*You shall receive power when the Holy Spirit
has come upon you; and you shall be my witnesses
in Jerusalem and in all Judea and Samaria and
to the end of the earth.* Acts 1:8

On Sunday morning, June 3, 1961 a fully loaded Boeing
707 jet was poised to begin its take-off run at Orly Airport
in Paris, France. The passengers were tourists returning to the United States after visiting the leading art cen-
ters of Europe. The usual flight apprehension had long
since been dissipated by the alluring fascination of smooth
and powerful jet travel. As the giant aircraft began to
gain momentum there were thoughts of home, memories
of a thousand satisfying experiences -- but few thoughts of
death!

Somewhere past the point of no return the captain applied all brakes and reversed the engines in an all-out
effort to stop the plane. For months afterward ominous
skid marks attested to the struggle for life as the plane
skidded off the end of the runway and exploded in flames.
One hundred and twenty six thousand pounds of jet fuel

created a funeral pyre for one hundred and twenty of the Atlanta area's most creative citizens.

Word of the tragedy struck an unbelieving Atlanta. Reality began to make its awesome and awful impression: power failure had brought death! Investigation of the accident later determined that there was an improper adjustment of the controls. The available power was not properly correlated to the needs of the moment. Tragedy was the result.

The aircraft industry has made unimaginable progress in the past fifty years. Tremendous loads can be lifted through the air. The largest jet engines have power equal to that of a diesel locomotive. The power was there. It was not adequately used.

It is ironic that we have been increasing our technological development of power while spiritual power is being neglected. Every aspect of our daily lives has increased in burdens, speed, and hazards. Yet we have either not begun our search for increased power to meet the demand or our search has been frustrated. As Saint Paul would say it, the world is too much with us.

OCCUPATIONS ARE TOO DEMANDING.

There was a time when the major vocational activity was agricultural. A person might work six days a week from dawn until dark and catch his/her rest by spending the day in church on Sunday. An occasional rainy day would break the spell of labor and remind him/her that the Creator was also working. Other persons were engaged in crafts and pursuits which were creative and satisfying to some degree. If a person accumulated wealth, that was good. But if he/she merely survived to rear a family, that was considered adequate.

Today the major vocational activity is abstract. Persons are dominated, even depersonalized, by machines. We are not as efficient as the machines which replace us. Those who do not have a highly developed skill or education may be known as "common labor." They were once called "hands." The dollar is the abstract symbol of human worth. And you know what is happening to the dollar!

For the affluent the situation is not much better. Wealth and status become ends in themselves. Many a man will sell his soul to make his wife a rich widow. Vance Packard, in his book, *The Status Seekers*, describes the ways in which the burdens of status and success-oriented living create intolerable pressures.

C. S. Lewis, in his *Screwtape Letters*, has the Devil describing the temptations of the relatively prosperous middle years of life:

> If on the other hand, the middle years prove prosperous, our position becomes even stronger. Prosperity knits a man to the world. He feels that he is "finding his place in it," while really it is finding its place in him. His increasing reputation, his widening circle of acquaintances, his sense of importance, the growing pressure of absorbing and agreeable work, build up in him a sense of really being at home in the earth, which is just what we want. (p. 143)

RECREATIONS ARE TOO ALLURING.

Considering the pressures of vocational life, there is a tremendous attraction in the relatively quiet spot on the lake, at the beach, or in the mountains. The country clubs build elaborate surroundings for our in-town retreats.

Spectator sports are in their most glamorous heyday. It appears that there never was a time when there was so much to do and so much money with which to do it. What would happen if a person had to choose between golf and God? People do it every day, you know.

MORAL DECISIONS ARE TOO COMPLEX.

Reinhold Niebuhr made it clear that in society we never have an absolute choice between pure truth and pure error. In society our relationships tend to become impersonal. The self-interest of races, corporations, and nations over-rides the individual. Although the decisions of personal morality may be less complex, the tremendous increase in privacy and mobility, the growing sense of moral relativity, and the corresponding dulling of moral perceptivity have created a situation of profound moral instability.

The prevailing undercurrent which is washing loose the foundations of morality and increasing the pressures of conformity is the "everybody does it" theme.

John Steinbeck, in *The Winter of Our Discontent*, portrays a community of "respectable" people whose moral patterns are guided by this maxim. One of the teenagers, Allen Hawley, is discovered to have won an essay contest by flagrant plagiarism. His reaction is not one of guilt or shame, but rather of intense anger at the person who called attention to his dishonesty. Allen's father tries vainly to help him see the wrongness of his action, only to be met by Allen's reply: "Who cares? Everybody does it. Don't you read the papers? Everybody does it -- right up to the top!"

Frank Gibney's study of white collar crime *(The Operators)* reveals the multi-billion dollar "take" of crime gone "respectable" and the respectable gone criminal. We have had to develop a new category of crime called the "victimless" crime. "Why not ease the penalties?" one asks. "Isn't everybody doing it?"

It no longer surprises me that significant numbers of church people use the same arguments to support legalized gambling, alcohol and drug legitimization, prostitution, and pornography -- to mention a few of our more obvious problems.

In a society of increased pressures such as this, one would expect that we would be alert to our need for increased power of will and moral perceptivity. The opposite seems to be the case. We live in a time when even the spiritual power of the past has been short-circuited by compromise, confusion, and neglect. We live in a time of power failure. The big jets advertised power to spare and met tragedy in one moment of failure. Perhaps we ought to learn a spiritual lesson from that experience.

WHEN POWER FAILS TRAGEDY IS ALWAYS THE RESULT.

Power failure brings out the more base instincts of the self. One of the reasons why the New York electricians' union has been able to win concessions beyond those anywhere else in America is that New York City does not dare to let the lights go out! A large city becomes like a jungle in the dark. Murder, theft, assault, and rape have become commonplace in our cities.

However, power failure leaves *each one* of us subject to the lesser demands of our existence. We become more concerned with ourselves than with the welfare of others. Littleness, bigotry, prejudice, and pride become characteristic of our relations with other persons and inhibit our relationship with God. Personal pleasures assume larger importance in our lives. Our moral perceptivity is dulled.

When power is restored, moral perceptivity is increased; and personal satisfactions are placed in the perspective of God's will.

WE MUST MAINTAIN FULL SPIRITUAL POWER IN OUR GENERATION.

The Apostle Peter wrote to the New Testament Church: "Be sure you keep your love for each other at full strength." (I Peter 4:8) No doubt he remembered Jesus' promise: "You shall receive power when the Holy Spirit has come upon you." The only adequate power for the living of these days is the power of the presence of God. The cultivation of a life of worship and prayer will reward you with the abundant life which Jesus came to make a vital reality for all who would follow him.

Do you have the spiritual power in your life which you know God wants you to have? The first step is an act of personal surrender to him in which you clarify your faith. The second step is to develop a pattern of meditation and prayer in which you are open to the attunement of God's presence in your life. And the third step is to keep on doing it!

Begin now.

5

THE LAST WORD

To Him who loves us and has freed us from our sins by His blood and made us a kingdom of priests to His God and Father, to Him be glory and dominion forever and ever.

Revelation 1:5b,6

We have two lovely daughters in our family. We named them Melody and Joy because we anticipated the beauty and satisfaction their presence would add to our home. We also have a son. Our son added an element of unpredictable adventure to our family life. It was not unusual to have dogs, cats, parakeets, fish, alligators, and frogs around the house during his childhood days. All that collecting of animals slowed down a bit after we lost one of the frogs in the house and spent an agonizing week hoping that no church members would visit until the fragrance of that dead frog was gone!

We tried to capitalize on our children's inquisitive spirits in order to further their knowledge of the world. One day our son brought in one of my shotgun shells and asked what was in it. We decided to cut into it and find out. We secured our best kitchen knife (the best kitchen

knife is most desirable for such projects) and cut through
the shell. We discovered how the shell contained pellets,
packing, and powder. The firing cap explodes the powder
-- which sends the pellets out of the barrel of the gun with
destructive force -- enough to kill a rabbit...or a person!
Even in this age of atomic weapons, gunpowder is more
destructive than any other force, because we are not
ashamed to use it.

This destructive use of gunpowder led Andre Maurois
to lament: "We owe to the middle ages the two worst in-
ventions of humanity -- gunpowder and romantic love." I
can easily understand how bad gunpowder has been. But
why is the same thing true of romantic love? I have always been in favor of it! One answer may be that in our
time love has been perverted -- particularly the highest
forms of human love. Love has been made identical with
sexuality, and sexuality has been made a matter of entertainment. Love has been objectified, and we live in an
era of "sex symbols" and "sex objects." Thus what is a
supremely beautiful human act has been reduced to an
animal function.

This perversion of the word love apparently caused
Aldous Huxley to say:
>Of all the worn, smudged, dog-eared words
>in our vocabulary, love is surely the grub-
>biest, smelliest, slimiest. Bawled from a
>million pulpits, crooned from a hundred
>million loudspeakers, it has become an out-
>rage to good taste and decent feeling -- an
>obscenity which one hesitates to pronounce.
>And yet, it has to be pronounced, for -- after
>all -- love is the last word.

Huxley is eminently correct. No matter how grubby,
how smelly, how slimy; no matter how besmirched in the
gutter love has become, it is the last word. That is the

word used by the Gospel. The good news of the Gospel is that the eternal God has loved us!

HE LOVED US.

There is no other word. God loves us! This was the best news pagans could hear. For them, the gods were capricious. They must be placated, sacrificed to and pleaded with. The Gospel of Jesus Christ is that God loves us. The sacrifice is his. The overcoming of the estrangement between us is something he has done. He loves us! We have not really begun to plumb the depths of meaning of that announcement.

Ironically, the people who are experiencing the bitterest dregs of life today are those who are most in position to realize the truth of the Gospel message: that although in this riddle of life there are no neat packaged answers, there is the assertion that God is still making his way through the thick of it with his love manifest in self-giving and suffering.

Love is the cement of all our congregational relationships. One of the best known and most appreciated stories is that of Ernest Freemont Tittle as minister of First United Methodist Church, Evanston, Illinois. Dr. Tittle applied the Gospel to life, not as imagined in somebody's dream world, but as it is in the market place, the factory, and the halls of politics. Consequently, just about everyone was aggravated with him. Management was against him. Labor was against him. The newspapers attacked him -- and last but not least, his Administrative Board was disturbed! The Board was on the point of requesting his resignation, when one of the most revered and influential men of the congregation rose to speak. He said, "As you all know, there is much which Dr. Tittle preaches which I cannot accept. But when my wife lay dying Dr. Tittle sat up all night with me. I love him. And as far as I am

concerned, he can preach in this church as long as he
wants!" Well, there was only silence -- and acceptance.
Dr. Tittle served as pastor of that church for some thirty
years after that -- and love was the leaven of his ministry
and his congregational relationship. Love will bind us together and make us effective in the world as nothing else
will. God has loved us!

HE HAS LOOSED US FROM OUR SINS.

The tendency for even the highest realities of human
life to become base and perverse indicates that persons
cannot release themselves from evil merely by good intention. Our highest moral accomplishments become instruments of sin. This is what Paul discovered in himself.
He called this the "curse of the law." The law, which was
the highest moral expression in history, including this
present time, became simply another device for distor-
ting the relationship between people and God. Thus Paul
saw that there is literally no way to escape from the bondage of sin by one's own efforts. This is what St. Augustine was later to call the "bound will."

Paul said, "I am carnal, sold under sin. I do not
understand my own actions. For I do not do what I want,
but I do the very thing I hate." (Romans 7:14, 15)

Further, he says, "I can will what is right, but I
cannot do it. For I do not do the good I want, but the evil
that I do not want is what I do."

And he concludes from this observation: "So I find it
to be a law that when I want to do right, evil lies close at
hand. For I delight in the law of God, in my inmost self,
but I see in my members another law at war with the law
of my mind and making me captive to the law of sin which
dwells in my members." (Romans 7:21 ff)

When Paul asks, "Who shall deliver me from this body of death?" he answers his own question with a triumphant exclamation, "Thanks be to God through our Lord Jesus Christ!....For the law of the Spirit of life in Christ Jesus has set me free from the law of sin and death." (Romans 7:25)

Sin is not merely something we do, it is actually a power which binds us and holds us. As Emil Brunner says, "We not only commit sins, we are sinners." There is no way to be released from that power except by the power of God himself. This is the triumphant news of the Gospel -- that God has broken the power of sin to hold us.

HE HAS MADE US A KINGDOM OF PRIESTS.

The Kingdom of God is the realm of God's victory over evil. Although there are areas in which natural evil has been overcome, the primary manifestation of the Kingdom of God is in the hearts of persons, and particularly those persons in whom the power of sin has been broken. If you have responded to the call of the Gospel, then you have become a part of God's kingdom. More especially you have become a kingdom of priests.

I am aware that many Protestants shy away from the word "priest." Others seem to be trying to forget that they are Protestants and use the term of their clergy. Neither of these approaches is the New Testament answer. We are all priests. We are what the word "priest" means -- "instruments of God." Some take the fact that we are all priests to suggest that each person approaches God directly in some sort of "buddy-buddy" fashion. No, the Protestant doctrine of the priesthood of all believers means that we are priest each to the other. We are God's instrument to be used by him in reaching our wife or husband, our child, our neighbor, our business associate, the stranger. God will use us -- if we will let him.

And God will use us regardless of any particular abilities which we may possess. I think I shall never forget the time my son and I attended the Roy Rogers Rodeo in Madison Square Garden in New York City. It was a rousing good show, full of excitement and fun. Right in the middle of the show after a demonstration of shooting targets thrown in the air, the lights of that great hall were dimmed and Roy and Dale rode their beautiful horses into the center of the arena. They told that audience of twenty-thousand people what Jesus Christ had done for them, and how they had given their hearts to Christ. It was a powerful Christian testimony. Then they sang a song which made chills run up and down my spine: "There Will Be Peace In The Valley For Me -- Some Day."

Later I came across a little book written by Dale Evans Rogers which indicates how this Christian experience of theirs came about. The book was titled *Angel Unaware*. It told the story of their mongoloid baby, Robin. In the book, Robin is back in heaven, and she is reporting to the Father of her "mission" to the world. Robin says, "Father, at first my parents were horror stricken that they had a 'retarded' baby. Even after we arrived home, I could see the struggle they were having to accept the way I was. Then, Father, I saw them begin to lean on you more and more. And I was so happy. I could not say anything or do anything. But I let your love shine through me all I could. Then I saw them surrender to you completely, and I knew my 'mission' was a success."

Dale Evans Rogers saw Robin as sent. I cannot believe that. I see nothing in the Gospels to cause me to believe that Robin was made deformed by God. But the condition being what it was, I believe Robin was *used* by God. And if God could use little Robin, with no abilities at all, think how much more he can use you and me if we but allow him to use us. He has made us a kingdom of priests. To him be glory and honor and majesty, forever.

6

A STANDARD OF MORALITY

Now therefore fear the Lord, and serve
him in sincerity and in faithfulness.
Joshua 24:14a

Fyodor Dostoevsky describes the nightmare world which would result from the dissolution of all moral standards. One of his characters in *Crime and Punishment,* Raskolnikov, dreamed that the whole world was condemned to a strange plague that had come to Europe from Asia. All were to be destroyed except a few persons. Microbes were attacking the bodies of persons. These things were spirits endowed with intelligence and will. People became at once mad and furious. . . .

Never had people considered themselves so intellectual and so completely in possession of the truth as these sufferers. Never had they considered their decisions, their scientific conclusions, their moral convictions so infallible. They did not know how to judge and could not agree what to consider evil and what good. They did not know whom to blame and whom to justify. Men killed each other

in a sort of senseless spite. All persons and things were
involved in destruction. The plague moved further and
further. . . .

We may now be living in just such a world as Dostoevsky
described. The dissolution of moral standards has the
world on the verge of its own destruction. We can't seem
to find a solution to the overwhelming problems of war,
famine, and greed. Recent events are the most blatant
indication that a threatened nation will violate the standards of international conduct upon which its own preser-
vation ultimately depends. When we consider the power
for self-destruction which rests at man's itchy trigger
finger, we begin to suspect that an adequate universal standard of morality is the only key to the world's survival.

AN ADEQUATE STANDARD OF MORALITY CANNOT BE
AN INDIVIDUAL STANDARD.

When persons and nations consider themselves ultimate in their judgment, decisions are no longer questioned, or are constantly questioned. We then lose our common
ground for communication and understanding. The avenues
for destruction become increasingly broad.

At a much less destructive level, this tendency to
make our own perceptions absolute has always been with
us. Have you ever noticed how, at baseball games, we
place every decision of the umpires under scrutiny of our
better vantage point -- a hundred feet away?

Wallace Hamilton told of an incident which occurred
when the great Walter Johnson was pitching for the Wash-
ington ball club. It is said that Johnson was so fast that
on a foggy day the ball was difficult to follow. On this particular day visual conditions were rather bad. Johnson
was burning his fast balls in. A rookie was at bat. He
stood in awe as strike one and strike two whizzed past him.

Johnson made his pitch, and the umpire shouted, "Strike three. You're out!" The rookie turned and said, "Did you see that ball, ump?" The umpire replied, "Well, no. But I heard it." The rookie replied, "I heard it too, and it sounded a little high to me!"

More to the point is the conversation among three umpires. The first umpire boasted, "I call 'em just like I see 'em." The second replied, "I call 'em the way they are." The third umpire said, "Heck, they ain't nothing 'til I call 'em!"

We are frighteningly to the place of the absolutizing of individual judgment. There are those who say, "Everyone has a right to his own opinion." Of course, that is true. But what if that opinion includes seducing your children or robbing your house? When we say, "Let everyone have his/her own opinion," we are usually assuming that everyone has a conscience which has been instructed by certain moral principles, such as the dignity of the person, the rights of the individual and respect for private property.

Immanual Kant stood at the dividing line between ancient and modern thought and expressed the view that every person has a sense of the "I ought" within him or her. Kant considered this a universal standard of duty. In our century, Emil Brunner asked, "What can 'Thou shalt' mean if it does not come from God? Who is the legislator that makes it right?" He observed that all too many people fall into the trap of identifying their inclination with their duty.

In his book, *Justice and the Social Order*, Brunner analyses what happens to the concept of justice when it loses its basis in the will of God. The age of rationalism explained the sense of justice in the human reason alone. The 19th century positivist philosophers denied God and

insisted that justice is purely relative, varying from one
place to another. It follows inevitably, insists Brunner,
that states will arise saying that the only justice is the
will of the ruling power. This reminds me hauntingly of
the thinking which concludes that the Constitution of the
United States is only what the Supreme Court says it is.
Hence, if there is no "sacred, eternal, divine absolute
law," it is impossible to denounce any law or national act
as unjust.

AN ADEQUATE STANDARD OF MORALITY CANNOT BE A DOUBLE STANDARD.

One standard of conduct for the rich and a different
one for the poor has been the breeding ground for injustice
in every era of history. The revolutionary spirit so alive
in our time is a rebellion against that very fact.

Neither is it acceptable to have one standard of business practices for workers and a different one for management. An article dealing with the degree of honesty
prevailing in America reported that the overwhelming majority of shoplifting in our stores is done by employees.
Employees felt that they were being overworked and under-
paid. They pointed to unscrupulous business methods as
a rationalization for their own dishonesty.

We have witnessed a bizarre attempt to overcome a
double standard of morality with regard to men and women.
As women have demanded equality in other areas of life,
so also have they demanded that the double standard of conduct be eliminated. The result has been disastrous! There
has been a general lowering of conduct. Neither "freedom"
nor "equality" is the culprit. Something is wrong with the
assumption that overcoming the double standard will be
beneficial. It has to do with the abortive nature of the
double standard itself.

Most of us have lived during the time when it was generally assumed (by whites!) that blacks would be less moral than whites. Court sentences reflected that assumption. Housing patterns and school populations were also influenced by it. Blacks and whites now see that assumption to be intolerable.

In all these cases: rich and poor, labor and management, male and female, black and white, a double standard of morality is a betrayer of justice, a destroyer of economic stability and a malignant moral force. A double standard, as also an individual standard, is no standard of morality at all!

AN ADEQUATE STANDARD OF MORALITY CANNOT BE A CULTURAL STANDARD.

Bernard Bell, in his book, *A Man Can Live*, describes the customs of the Igorot Tribe in northern Luzon. The custom in that tribe required that any youth desiring adult status should go out on a dark night, waylay some unsuspecting traveler, cut off his head and impale it on a stake in front of his hut. This act was an announcement to the tribe that he was now ready for adult responsibilities. It was the ethical requirement of the community.

We may be horrified with the level of morality of that tribe -- but who is to say they are wrong? Many persons today assert that the morality of a culture is *right* for that culture -- without regard to the nature or the consequences of the act.

Perhaps you are ready to allow a relative morality for the Igorots of northern Luzon. But are you willing to affirm it for the changing assumptions of your own children?

Television programs do more to imprint cultural assumptions on the minds of people than any other force in our time. We have translated freedom of speech into an insidious cultural influence. We are in a time when freedom of speech calls for moral responsibility more forcefully, precisely because of the cultural impact of the media. Someone once said that freedom of speech does not give one the right to shout"Fire!" in a burning building. Make no mistake, our culture is in moral chaos and a very small group of people have an inordinate influence on the public mind. What they "shout" should reflect the highest level of social responsibility.

Cultural morality victimizes the church's perception of the will of God. Have you noticed how many different perceptions of the will of God address any particular social problem? I was appalled in my early ministry to discover that things in the New Testament which seemed to address the issue of race relations clearly and unequivocally were often interpreted in an entirely different way by different Christian groups.

So long as the interpretation of the New Testament stays within the prescribed bounds of our culturally accepted patterns, there is little prospect of change. The actual standard in that case is not the will of God but the cultural perception of it. As is the case with the individual and double standards, a cultural standard of morality is, in the final analysis, no standard at all.

What we must have is a standard of morality which transcends the individual, the group, and the culture. Whether it has been seen as the revealed will of God, universal moral law, or the "unalienable rights of man," human society has been and still is basing its hope upon a sensitivity to a moral claim which transcends any one individual, group, or culture.

The wellsprings of our Judeo-Christian history flow into the present. The roots of our awareness run deep.

Joshua already knew that life demanded a choice, between emergent cultural gods and the very Source of his existence, the God who had made himself known in Israel's brief history. His alternative should still be ringing in our ears:

> ...fear the Lord and serve him in sincerity and faithfulness; put away the gods which your fathers served beyond the River.... And if you be unwilling to serve the Lord, choose this day whom you will serve.... But as for me and my house, we will serve the Lord.
>
> (Joshua 24:14, 15)

Quite simply, it is a matter of choice. But some standards cannot be satisfying because they are self-defeating. When we respond to God, our decisions may still be complex, frustrating, and difficult. But at least we have a sense of direction and a hope for survival.

7

ARE BETTER DAYS AHEAD?

*"I consider that the sufferings of this
present time are not worth comparing with the
glory that is to be revealed to us."*
Romans 8:18

"There is a madness loose in the world, and it plays
havoc with individuals and institutions alike." This was
the alarming observation with which Hal Gulliver began
his editorial in the Atlanta Constitution for this past Thurs-
day. His comment referred to the attempted assassination
of Pope John Paul II on Wednesday, just a few weeks after
the attempt on President Reagan's life. No one at the center of public life is safe because there is no way he or she
can be adequately protected in a free society.

The result of this awareness is the suspicion that if
they are not safe, then *no one* is safe! There is a tremendous undercurrent of insecurity eroding the foundations of
our emotional and material well-being. This sense of insecurity is enhanced by seemingly unsolvable problems in
Northern Ireland. The Middle East is a powder keg --just
waiting to explode. Our own government officials are now

51

admitting that time is running out for a peaceful solution
to the present crisis. Although global war is unthinkable
today, we know we can drift into it as local conflicts draw
others into the pattern of violence.

Adding to our sense of insecurity is the economic situation in the United States. It is so complex, and so involved with political vested interests, that steps to correct
one weakness threaten others. Just at the time when the
president and the congress agree on a course of action which
the business community seems to want, the stock market
drops sixty points! As one commentator observed, "If there
is a key to the stock market decline, it is 'uncertainty.'"

That which is true on the international and national
scene is also true for us as individuals. The future can
be tremendously threatening! For the teen-ager today the
future may be so obscure or seemingly hopeless as to make
life in the present unendurable. The middle-aged person
may feel in his/her bones that his best days are behind
him. That can be devastating to his/her creative thrust
and zest for living. The elderly person may see only the
prospect of increased loneliness and bodily infirmity. Such
a prospect can become a spectre of anxiety, vitiating the
satisfactions of the present and poisoning the memories of
the past.

The constant question -- sometimes vividly conscious
and at other times gnawingly unconscious -- is this: are
better days ahead?

We awaken one morning to the awareness of a suspi-
cious lump in our body. A mysterious pain in the chest
stabs us into alertness. We wonder how we shall make it
to the end -- whether we shall keep our economic viability,
or, worse still, our dignity. From every quarter the re-
curring stimuli of our environment cause us to wonder:
what is going to happen to us?

It would be wonderful if we could announce the certainty, or even the probability, that the world will be a better place in the future. The nineteenth century evolutionary assurances of inevitable progress have been dashed on the rocky shore of reality. There is every indication that disease, war, and terrorism will continue to ravage human existence.

We live in a world where greed gains the technocratic expertise to manipulate persons by the millions, where war has become a way of life and where a knowledgeable and sensitive person could easily fall into an abyss of despair.

If there is one person who ought to be able to avoid that abyss, it is the Christian. The long view of our history is speaking to us. The words are those of the Apostle Paul:

> I consider that the sufferings of this present
> time are not worth comparing with the glory
> that is to be revealed to us. For the crea-
> tion waits with eager longing for the reveal-
> ing of the (children) of God.... We know that
> in everything God works for good with those
> who love him, who are called according to
> his purpose.

This is the same ringing optimism which John sounded in the book of Revelation. He was writing to Christians whose lives were threatened by an ultimate terrorism. Not only were their lives threatened, the future of their world offered no promise. The Christian movement itself was in jeopardy.

Paul and John proclaim in the harmony of one voice: God is sovereign! He will be victorious over the powers of evil! In every circumstance he is working for good with those who love him, who are called according to his purpose!

This particular Pauline passage has been one of the most difficult for me to understand or accept over the years. It always seemed to carry a note of fatalism which surrounded evil circumstances with a halo of divine intention. The King James translation expressed this meaning in a form I could not reconcile with the love of God in Jesus Christ and with the tragic facts of human existence. There are some things which *cannot* be called good in themselves. Nor could anything but a *tour de force* make them appear to be good in some overall plan.

The Revised Standard translation makes the meaning clearer. To know that God is at work in the midst of every evil, however tragic the circumstance, is tremendously encouraging to me. The evil in the world does not change to good merely because we love God. It is important to realize that the realities remain what they are. Something, however, has changed -- and changed marvelously. The tragic circumstances have lost their power to defeat us!

Surely something like that was what Ralph Waldo Emerson had in mind when he said, "This time, like all times, is a very good one if we but know what to do with it." One thing we Christians must have learned from our history is to trust our times into the hands of God. The future belongs to him and we belong to him. For Paul the very creation itself was waiting with eager longing for the children of God to come into their own! Better days *are* ahead!

BETTER DAYS ARE AHEAD -- FOR PERSONS OF DEDICATION.

The Gospel assures a better day for persons of faith. Not, to be sure, a fatalistic faith that everything is inexorably worked out in a total plan of God. Rather, it is an awareness that God's presence and power are available to us in our daily lives. God is cooperating *with* those who love him.

Sometimes we tend to forget that the achievement of good is God's purpose. We ascribe to his will events and circumstances which in any other view would be undeniably characterized as evil. Evil in the world is neither the will of God nor the work of God. Jesus at least made that clear.

God has used the Church as his instrument of goodness in spite of its own hypocrisies and weaknesses. Possibly the greatest miracle of all is that the Church has been of any use to him at all. Yet at a time when so many are predicting the demise of the Church, I see a new thrust of dedication, a new power of the institution to make a difference in the world. One has only to see what the Church is doing in Poland and Latin America to understand that dedication can make a total difference in the future. I am not as confident of the Church in the United States, but the long view of our Christian history assures me that it *can* make a difference!

BETTER DAYS ARE AHEAD -- FOR PERSONS OF DE-
    TERMINATION.

Better days are ahead for those who are willing and who know how to cooperate with God. There are those who will make better days by the power of their own determination.

I can hardly wait for the day when J. R. Richard pitches baseball again for the Houston Astros. Last summer Richard suffered a massive stroke. Doctors feared that he would never walk again -- much less play baseball. That was out of the question. But not for Richard. He has been relentless in his determination to play again. Even now he pitches batting practice. Whether he will be effective as a pitcher again, I do not know. But the miracle has already taken place. The miracle is in his heart!

Who would have thought that Franklin Delano Roosevelt would have better days after he was stricken with polio? How easy it would have been for him to conclude that God intended for him a life of semi-retirement at his Hyde Park home! Yet by the power of intense determination he achieved the presidency of this country and directed the course of our nation through one of the most crucial periods in our history.

Better days are possible even for those who are reduced to the minimum of human function. Betsy Barton was another victim of polio. Her situation appeared much more desperate than that of Roosevelt. She could literally do nothing but breathe. One day her neighbor said to her, "If breathing is all you can do, let's begin with that." He taught her how to breathe correctly. Then he taught her how to move her stomach muscles. From those two simple exercises Betsy built her muscular coordination. Later she said, "Upon those two exercises hung my health. With these two simple things as rungs, I started to climb the ladder of strength, to win back my life." Betsy Barton lived to see better days.

BETTER DAYS ARE AHEAD -- FOR PERSONS OF DISCIPLINE.

Dedication and determination are the fabric of discipline -- the way dedication is expressed, the way determination comes to fruition.

It is in the arena of discipline that the individual's will to live is tested. Discipline focuses the energies of institution or nation into creative purpose.

Discipline can bring a nation back to economic and moral health. A nation wracked with discontent, demoralized by self-interest and infected with drug abuse is in a poor state to contribute to its own well-being or that of the world. In World War II General Hague was commenting on an attack he was about to make on a strongly established position. He said, "Now it will be seen what those defenses will be worth when manned by troops no longer resolved to defend them."

The Church has been a bulwark of this nation's strength for two hundred years. We are still strong. But the feeling of insecurity is pervasive. Better days are ahead for the Church only if the strands of dedication and determination can be woven into the strong cord of discipline.

We need a new cohesiveness not born of likeness but of likemindedness. That mind must be the mind of Christ.

When worship is an attempt to see the mind of Christ;

when giving is an expression of overflowing gratitude;

when priorities reflect sensitivity to human need;

when "survival" gives way to service;

when we know and follow him who is in command;

when discipline does not tolerate laxity of duty;

then better days are ahead!

8

THE INDELIBLE IMPRESSION

I have learned to be content whatever the circumstances.   Philippians 4:11
                                                (Phillips)

Saint Paul referred to himself as a "man in Christ." The impact of the encounter with Christ on the Damascus Road was life-transforming for him. Most of us do not meet Christ on some visionary Damascus Road. We meet him in the life and witness of persons. Many persons influenced my life in the direction of the Lord, and I am thankful for each one of them. However, there is usually *one* person who makes that indelible mark which stays with us forever.

A standard feature of The Reader's Digest for many years is titled, "The Most Unforgettable Character I've Met." The articles have told the stories of some remarkable human beings. Some of them have changed the direction of history. In the June, 1951 issue, the article described a man named Bruce. The author, Bryan Collier, begins by saying:

This article could not have been written while
Bruce lived because he would have been em-
barrassed. Yet if this blithe spirit were peer-
ing over my shoulder now, I think he would be
wearing the old familiar smile. He was an
exceedingly able newspaperman and, deep inside, he certainly knew that his was a remarkable story of stark courage, tough as rawhide.

I share this story with you today with the hope that
you, as I and many others have done, will see the face of
Christ in him. His life is an illustration of the words of
Paul: "I have learned, in whatever the circumstances, to
be content."

I have learned...

Bruce's life was, more than most, a continual learning process. A deteriorating physical condition forced
him to learn increasingly difficult lessons of adjustment
to the circumstances of life. One person described him:
Nothing but a great big heart and a mind
with a remarkably retentive memory, a
monumental capacity for knowledge and
understanding, and a distressingly small
handful of skin and bones.

This "remarkably retentive mind" was the result of
years of concentration and learning. Bruce knew very early
in life that his body would be of little use to him. He learned to depend upon his mind.

Let me describe how Bruce lived. Physically, he
was totally helpless. He could move his hands to the wrist
and his head at the neck. *Nothing else*. He could sometimes drag his arm from the arm of his chair to an adjoin-
ing table by letting his fingers do the walking along the arm
of the chair or across the table.

When one is totally helpless merely arranging the mechanics of living is an almost impossible task. Bruce could not move his wheelchair an inch without help. His food and drink were brought to him. His body would be placed in a leaning position above the plate. He could then feed himself by the movement of his wrist.

At his work Bruce's chair was attached to the desk so that it would not move. By manipulating his fingers he could move his hands in a quarter circle about the desk. By this method he could edit the news copy which was brought to him. His hands developed thick calluses from friction with the desk. At his hotel porters did *everything* for him. This is the way he lived. He learned his routine well and lived completely by it.

whatever the circumstances...

As a child Bruce was robust and healthy. When he was three or four years of age his parents noticed that he had difficulty lifting his arms. His physical deterioration continued, so that by the age of twelve he could walk only by flinging himself forward in a grotesque attempt to maintain his balance. His balance was so precarious that he fell often and hard. His attempt to use crutches proved futile -- his walking days were over.

Bruce went through high school in a wheelchair. Willing friends pushed him from place to place and lifted him over barriers and obstacles and up steps. He was never without a helping hand. When he was determined to go to college in 1936 there was no money. No one could imagine that he could adjust to the conditions of dormitory living. Yet no one had the heart to keep him from trying. So -- he went to the University of Georgia. Four years of perseverance, and hundreds of willing hands, brought him to the reward of a degree in journalism.

Bruce found ample reason to ask himself: "What good is a college degree if no one will give you a chance?" Due to World War II most of the able-bodied men were in military service or otherwise employed. Finally, the editor of the Columbus (Georgia) Ledger, desperate for help, hired him, sight unseen, on the recommendation of Dean Drewry of the University of Georgia School of Journalism. Collier recalled the moment:

> I shall never forget the day he arrived. I
> looked up from some work as he was wheeled
> into my office, and tried to mask my shock.
> Every part of his body was devastated and
> skeletonized -- every part except his face.
> I still don't know why I refrained from say-
> ing at once: "Look, Bruce, I'm sorry, but
> you cannot possibly do the work I want
> done." But I didn't say it.

Later the managing editor of the newspaper reported: "I do not understand it. But Bruce is handling more copy, and handling it better, than anyone else on the desk." In six years he was the associate editor of the newspaper.

> Collier said of him:
> Strangely, he was never ill, though always
> he was dying. He had muscular dystrophy,
> a progressive disease as hopeless as can-
> cer in its last stages. Bruce was like this.
> He knew all along that he was doomed. His
> close friends knew that he was marked. But
> he looked at it objectively, like the good
> newspaperman he was. He weighed the sit-
> uation, calculated the probable end, and then
> coolly filed the information in the inner re-
> cesses of his mind.

In the spring of 1948 Bruce had been told by his doctor that he ought to make some plans — whatever plans a person may make who knows that his next visitor is death. He informed his editor of the situation and requested that he be allowed to continue his work. In the summer of 1950 Collier was in Bruce's room and asked, "What's the dope, Bruce?" He smiled and said, "I am still kicking around. I am surprised and happy every morning when I wake up. "

On March 8, 1951, Bruce said good-bye to his friends and went home to be with his family. Two days later the words moved across the country by teletype: Bruce ... dead at thirty-two of muscular dystrophy.

to be content.

Bruce's was not the contentment of hopelessness, resignation or despair. His was the same contentment as that of Paul as he bore his "thorn in the flesh." Bleak despair never touched him. If bitterness, frustration, or fear ever fringed momentarily upon his questing for knowledge or his compulsions for service, he flung them aside quickly. Collier said of him:

> For a man with no mortal future, he was
> keenly interested in that of others. For a
> man with so little hope, he instilled hope
> and confidence among his friends.

The worn-out Gideon Bible on his hotel desk attested to the source of Bruce's inner strength. His was a contentment in Christ, arising out of a profound confidence in the love of God. It was a contentment which left him free to wring the most out of life and to make his greatest contribution to life.

Three days before his death Bruce wrote an editorial about the plans of the Jewish organization, B'Nai B'Rith, to do research on muscular dystrophy. He called it "Medicine's Last Blind Alley." "Muscular dystrophy," he wrote, "is a disease as hopeless as cancer in its last stages, which means that there is no retreat from it save death." His appeal for research was his last act. Yet there was no hint that he was doomed by medical science's lagging efforts.

Neither Bruce's life nor his premature death were tragic. Rather, they were victorious. And the triumph of his unobtrusive witness marked many a life with the stamp of an inveterate optimism called faith. Those who knew him were fortunate beyond measure. I consider myself most fortunate of all. He was my brother.

9

NONE SO BLIND

*Jesus said (to Bartimaeus), "What do you
want me to do for you?" And the blind man said
to him, "Master, let me receive my sight." And
Jesus said to him, "Go your way; your faith has
made you well."*

                                    Mark 10:51-52

This passage of scripture reads differently for a
child than for an adult. Children might ask, "Was the
blind man really healed?" We adul's might reply, "Well
...uh..." We have been conditioned by the modern scientific view to think that the healing is unlikely -- and so we
skim over the event in order to keep the Bible's credibili-
ty and our credulity in shouting distance of one another.
How easily we slide through these monumental events in
the life of humanity. Because they are inconceivable to
us, we overlook them -- and they *are* inconceivable to us!

But what if *we* were the blind man? Can *you* put
yourself in Bartimaeus' place?

"Bartimaeus, a blind beggar, the son of Timaeus,
was sitting in his usual place by the side of the road.

When he heard that it was Jesus, he began to call out,
'Jesus, Son of David, have pity on me!'"

Can you put yourself in this scene? Have you ever
had to beg for anything? Really beg? To beg in that ser-
vile way that robs one of his dignity as a human being?

There is a great deal of force in that phrase "his
usual place." We have a way in society of separating and
categorizing persons, in cultural terms, in economic and
racial terms, and in terms of age and sex so that we can
become terribly alienated from one another. Bartimaeus
sat in his usual place by the side of the road. Because of
his handicap he was pushed to the periphery of vital life,
of meaningful activity. Bartimaeus was not like Sam
Walter Foss who said, "Let me live in my house by the
side of the road, and be a friend to man." That is the ide-
alistic view of it. Bartimaeus was sitting in the dirt! He
felt the sting of the grains of sand as scuffling children and
thoughtless travelers hurried past. He was pushed out,
ignored, forgotten.

Perhaps we are getting a little closer to Bartimaeus.
I listen to many elderly persons who feel pushed out, ignored, and forgotten. The retirement problem is not so
much the change in work habits. It is the not-too subtle
suggestion that we have been relegated to the edge of productive life.

It may be that children and young people feel this
most poignantly. For a teenager to be pushed out of a
group which he/she values is an agonizing experience. Do
you remember how it felt as a child to be excluded from a
game which the other children were playing?

For Bartimaeus, survival depended upon his ability
to persuade a busy and callous world to notice him. Help
the blind!" "Help the blind!" Everyone was accustomed

to hearing that shout. Occasionally someone would toss
a coin his way, and Bartimaeus would eagerly dig it out
of the dirt. Bartimaeus the animal survived. Bartimaeus
the man shriveled.

Thus Bartimaeus became a crafty adapter to the
manipulative ways of human intercourse. He had learned
to traffic in gossip, selling information for a few coins
now and then. He had heard of the miracle-workings of
one Jesus of Nazareth. He had looked to healers all his
life, but none of them had ever paid him any attention.

This time, when the sound of the crowd and the all-
too-familiar sting of the sand shocked Bartimaeus into
alertness, he heard that Jesus of Nazareth was coming
his way. He cried out, "Jesus, son of David, have pity
on me!" When the crowd tried to quiet him, he shouted
all the more: "Jesus, have mercy on me!" Then Jesus
stopped. The crowd fell silent, because no healer had
ever paid the slightest attention to the beggar, Bartimaeus.

In that pregnant silence, the crowd waited to see
what would happen. But their minds raced on ahead of
them. I can imagine what they may have been thinking:
What does Bartimaeus want now? Surely he does not want
his sight! Then he would have to work like the rest of us.
Bartimaeus doesn't know what a good thing he has. All he
has to do is sit all day and feed on the generosity of those
of us who are productive!

Jesus broke the silence and said, "What do you want
me to do for you?" Bartimaeus replied, "Oh Master, let
me see again!" Jesus said, "Go on your way, then. Your
faith has healed you." Bartimaeus immediately received
his sight and began to follow Jesus.

I suspect that a good many more people would begin
to follow Jesus, and *all of us* would follow him more

closely, if we could just be healed of our blindness. Mark it well: We are *all* Bartimaeus! The question is not that of a remote miracle in the first century. The question is what we are going to do with our lives in the twentieth century.

YOU AND I ARE BLIND BECAÚSE WE CANNOT SEE.

As children of the modern age we have been conditioned not to "see" anything which does not make sense to us. This is the unfortunate legacy of the "age of reason."

The European metaphysical clown, Karl Valentin, makes this point hilariously clear. The clown appears on stage with a quizzical look on his face. He is in front of a house, and the only light is that of the dim street light. He looks around on the ground as though he has lost something. Crowd expectation increases as he searches diligently under the light.

A police officer walks past. Seeing the man engaged in a search, the police officer without a word joins in the search. After a while, the officer asks, "What did you lose?" The clown replies, "I lost the key to my house." "Oh," says the officer, and they continue to search.

Finally, the officer asks, "Are you sure you lost it here?" "Oh, no," says the clown. "I lost it over there." (as he points to a darker part of the stage) Exasperated, the officer asks, "Then why are you looking over here?" With superior self-assurance the clown replies, "Because the light is better over here!"

The children of my generation have lived to see the absurdity of persons looking desperately for the key to their eternal house under the dim streetlights of their reason when they lost that key in the dark labyrinths of the human soul which reason cannot fathom. We have seen philosophers insist that the only meaningful sentences were declaratory sentences of defined terms, leaving to mere opinion the highest expressions of human love and the noblest expressions of human aspiration.

Not merely have we labored under the restricted vision of a limited scientific method, we have experienced the limited vision of our cultural conditioning. We are woefully unprepared and ill-equipped to understand persons of other cultures in the world. We blot other people out, at home and abroad, by putting distance between us. We do not abandon neighborhoods because they deteriorate. Neighborhoods deteriorate because we abandon them. Sometimes we wonder why we can't see the fact. The reason lies in another of our human proclivities -- the tendency to rationalize our conduct.

WE ARE BLIND BECAUSE WE WILL NOT SEE.

I can identify with the fellow who went to his optometrist and said, "I would like to see things a little less clearly, please." There are so many problems in the world that it would be a relief not to see some of them. A good many of us seem to react to the world in that way. Mathew Henry in the seventeenth century said, "There is none so blind as he who will not see." All of us have that problem when it comes to our particular vested interests.

A good friend of mine had more than one personal problem. However, two of her problems had to do with the fact that she was diabetic and greatly overweight. Her weight aggravated her diabetes. Yet all her efforts at dieting seemed, if anything, to be counterproductive.

One day I walked into the room where she was sitting, stuffing herself with a chocolate eclair. (Of course there is no other way to eat a chocolate eclair. One is *committed* with the first bite. After that it is a race to keep up with the chocolate and the cream filling which squashes out the side of your mouth!)

I had never commented on her weight before. I had always chosen rather to commiserate with her on other subjects. This time, however, I said, "Why are you stuffing yourself?" She replied innocently, "Well, I *take* my insulin."

We human beings have a marvelous capacity to see what we want to see, hear what we want to hear, and do what we really want to do! Whether we are motivated by fear or desire, we can always explain our conduct. This is true whether it involves getting a loved one who has life-threatening symptoms to see a doctor or convincing the cocktail set that alcohol is a more dangerous drug in American society than heroin, cocaine, or marijuana. Confront me at the point of my vested interests and I *will* be blind!

WE ARE BLIND BECAUSE WE SEE TOO MUCH.

Have you ever met a car on a curve at night and its high beam blinded you? You were seeing too much light. Have you ever turned on the lights in the middle of the night and had to wait until your eyes adjusted before you could see? You were seeing too much light. Do you have red flags which irritate you or pet peeves which bother you? On those instances you may be seeing too much.

As children we used to play a game in which we would spin round and round until the whole world would become a blur. We were seeing too much. Sometimes early childhood experiences create emotional wounds which leave scars to affect our perception for the rest of of our lives.

Perception is warped for people of all races in a
racist society. Perception is warped for people of both
sexes in a sexist society. Perception is warped for people whose prejudices are formed by sectional bias.

Lewis Grizzard described a perfect example of
this blindness which occurred in New York City during the
Democratic National Convention. A former Georgian,
well educated, cultured, and living in New York, double-
parked her new Mercedes in front of a private residence.
The car, for irrelevant reasons, carried Georgia license
plates. When she returned to her car she found this note:

> You good ol' boys from Georgia are all
> alike. Next time, why don't you do us a
> big favor and double-park your Mercedes
> somewhere on Peachtree Street and *leave
> it there!*
> I am sick and tired of you drawling coun-
> try hicks and your stupid drawling presi-
> dent and his stupid drawling brother. I
> don't think I can wait until you are finally
> out of town.
> > Signed: An extremely irritated
> > New Yorker

It hurts to be victimized by someone else's blindness. But as Bartimaeus could tell us, it hurts even
more to be victimized by *our own* blindness.

As the Lord confronted Bartimaeus, he said, "What
do you want me to do for you?" That is what he says to
each one of us. Every day brings the Lord's question to
my mind: "Garnett, what do you want me to do for you
today?" And in my better moments I reply, "Master,
just let me see again. Help me to see myself more clearly.
Help me to see others more clearly. Make me a more
perceptive, more sensitive, more mature human being;

overcome the barriers which separate me from people;
overcome the stereotypes which blind me to their needs,
their hopes, their pain. And having seen, make me an
instrument of your peace."

10

ONCE MORE -- WITH FEELING

One came up to (Jesus), saying, "Teacher,
what good deed must I do, to have eternal life?"
                                      Matthew 19:16

A man came to Jesus and asked him, "What good
deed must I do to inherit eternal life?" When a person
asks about eternal life he is not just passing the time of
day. Someone has observed that every question is a statement. The question about eternal life is the ultimate
statement: We were meant for more than this earthly life
indicates. This is true whether one examines the practices of the cultures of history or whether one deals with
the individual aspirations of persons.

This is usually called the story of the rich young
ruler. All accounts of the story present the man as rich
and Luke calls him a ruler. Matthew calls him a young
man. When we get the whole picture from Matthew, Mark,
and Luke we see an older man, a community leader, a man
of wealth and highly respected. His mind told him he was
respectable. He could think of no commandment he had

not diligently tried to keep. His community told him he was an achiever. Persons spoke well of him. They entrusted him with the greater decisions of the community. But his deep inner longing told him that his life was incomplete. He needed something.

Mark and Luke may be more accurate in their account. They portray Jesus defining his need. Jesus said, "You lack one thing." But Matthew may be more to the point. When Jesus talks to him about keeping the commandments, the man replies, "I have kept these all my life. What do I still lack?" Here is a good person by all the standards we know. Yet he is not satisfied with his life. Nor has conventional religion been of much help, at least to his feeling. Something is gnawing deep within him.

Presumably this man enjoyed all the pleasures and comforts which wealth in those days could acquire. Closer to our own time, Friedrich Nietzsche put it succinctly: "Pleasure wants eternity, deep, deep eternity." In every age there has been the suspicion that there *has* to be something more!

Apparently this man hoped to receive something new and different from Jesus -- some new command, a "brilliant fresh departure in religion." And all that Jesus told him was what he already knew!

I think our biggest contemporary problem among Christian people, not to mention the population at large, is that we have a suspicion that there is more to life than we are getting. Yet we consider that the ordinary commandments, the conventional religion, is inadequate. It does not seem to occur to us that the religious vacuum is *our* fault. God tells us what to do and we say, "Lord, you *know* I can't do that. What do you want me to do *less* than that?" And the Lord says nothing. The silence of God, the absence of God, the so-called death of God is a judgment upon our equivocating ways.

Jesus looked at the man and loved him. I have seen so many wonderful people, tremendous people, people who knew better and longed for more of what God wants us all to have, who simply would not respond to the clearly delineated claims of the Gospel. I have sat for hours counseling with a man who in my opinion had all the qualities of sensitivity and compassion of a saint. Yet he was having an affair with another man's wife and he would not give her up. He was trying to satisfy his longing for eternal life by the stimulation of illicit adventure.

There is no pleasure -- no pleasure that is not in the end a dead-end street and at best the suggestion of an eternal pleasure. Nietzsche said it: "Pleasure wants eternity, deep, deep eternity!"

In the late Middle Ages the longing for eternity often expressed itself in mysticism. Exhaustive, sometimes bizarre attempts were made to climb the mystical ladder to God. Today it is called "mind expansion." The mysticism is more likely to be of the Eastern atheistic type, in which the person seeks to achieve some form of self-transcendence. We have seen desperate attempts in our time to break out beyond the self, from sniffing glue to LSD. The drug culture has become the camp meeting of the latter half of the twentieth century. More traditional forms of this search are the house church, the Bible study group, and the charismatic movement. "I am not being fed" is the lament of a person who is about to be on the move spiritually. Sometimes the move takes absolutist, cocksure, bigoted forms. When the need becomes desperate we must have *all* the answers.

A few years ago there was a play on Broadway in New York City titled "Once More -- With Feeling!" The play title was a take-off on a show-business cliché. In rehearsals, after everything is perfected, the director will say, "All right, let's do it once more -- this time with feeling." To be converted again is not really such a bad idea. The great missionary E. Stanley Jones once observed that most people need re-birth in their forties on general principles.

Many of us have grown away from the vitality of our religious experience. We can identify with Lord Byron's lament:

> I now have ashes where once I had fire,
> The soul in my body is dead;
> The thing I once loved, I now merely admire,
> My heart is as gray as my head.

Others of us cannot *recall* any particularly vital experience of the Lord. Of course it is not by any means necessary, nor even desirable, that we should be converted in any stereotyped sense. We do not have to have a Damascus Road type experience such as Paul had. Nor do we have to have some earthshaking encounter with the Lord. But we *do* have to know where we stand with the Lord. We have to know if we love him, if we are surrendered to him.

This is what being "born again" means. It means knowing that Jesus is *your* Lord. This is the catch. There are people who seem to *know* it better than we do. And they can make us feel terribly guilty! Many of us can identify with the man who came to Jesus as we say, "Lord, convert me once more -- *this time* with feeling!"

We see someone who shows more outward signs of feeling the presence of God than we do -- or talks more intimately about the Holy Spirit than we do -- and we begin to feel inadequate or threatened, or both. Have you ever had anyone to put you on the defensive by the way he or she talked about the Holy Spirit? That may not be all bad. You may *need* to be more surrendered to the Lord. But only you and the Lord know that. What is bad is when the search for feeling becomes an end in itself.

SOME PEOPLE ATTEND CHURCH TO GET A GOOD FEELING.

I can see a strong tendency in our present society to let feeling become an end in itself. There are those who do not think that they have truly worshiped if they do not "get high" or have an emotional time of it.

Charles Merrill Smith wrote a humorous, tongue-in-cheek book titled *How to Become a Bishop Without Being Religious*. The book presumes to tell the ambitious young preacher how to get ahead without being truly devoted to God by playing to the wishes of the congregation. Smith says, "What there is a market for is 'subjective worship.' This is the type of worship which has as its goal the creation of certain states of feeling in the worshiper." He suggests that the aspiring preacher play heavily on nostalgia and sentimental music. "Such a preacher," says Smith, "never lets (people's) attention stray from themselves, which is the subject, he knows, in which they are most vitally interested."

Self-centered worship will always be feeling-oriented.

OTHER PEOPLE DECRY THE FEELING EMPHASIS AND REACT NEGATIVELY TO IT.

These people do not want to have anything to do with nostalgia, the gospel song set, or the charismatic movement. They want quietness, with as little emotional expression as possible. Anything that shows freedom in worship smacks of frivolity to them. Liturgy must be formal, highly structured, and dignified. Songs like "In the Garden" or "Blessed Assurance" become "bad" hymns.

Of course, this is a reaction to the other extreme. It is easy to miss something vital about the Christian experience in this reaction. There is no guideline, biblical or otherwise, which says that the experience of Christ or the expression of worship has to take any certain form.

CHRIST WANTS YOU TO HAVE A GOOD FEELING.

It is impossible to imagine any experience of the Ultimate, or what concerns us ultimately, which does not bring about *some* emotional response. Christ wants you to have a good feeling,
> not as an end in itself,
> nor as an exercise in nostalgia
> or self-worship,
> but in the sense of love offered,
>> forgiveness given,
>> and your being affirmed.

When John Wesley "felt his heart strangely warmed," it was because he fully realized in that moment that Christ did love him and loved him completely. That awareness will make anyone feel good!

When you or I fully realize that the power of sin over us has been broken by the power of God himself, that awareness will make us feel good!

And when we realize that we are *really* important to God, our self-image will be strengthened. When our self-image is strengthened, we will not *have* to have all the answers any more. Our act of faith will cease to be a desperate act of an insecure person in a panic civilization. It will then become the "assurance of things hoped for, the conviction of things not seen."   (Hebrews 11:1)

11

THE JOY OF BEING CHOSEN

You did not choose me, but I chose you
and appointed you that you should go and bear
fruit and that your fruit should abide ...

John 15:16a

Can you remember as a child what a joy it was to be chosen? When they were choosing sides for a game, do you remember how the suspense would build toward the end of the selection process? Finally they would lump two or three kids together to finish out the sides. That meant that they were not skilled enough to be chosen. Humiliating! In school it was a great ego stimulant to be chosen by the teacher for a part in a play, or even to dust the erasers. It never occurred to some of us boys that perhaps the teacher wanted us out of the room for a while! The worst agony of all was wondering whether the girl we chose to ask for a date would choose us in return. There is something tremendously self-affirming about being chosen. That instinct may be congenital. At least it goes back a long way in our cultural past.

Most of us do not go back so far in our awareness of those choices which made us who we are and what we are. We cannot trace the memory of those who chose for their progeny to live in America. Alex Haley recognized this inveterate need for roots. He became so obsessed with the question of his ancestry that he took the faintest threads of memory and traced them painstakingly over the years to a tribe in the Zambia River Valley in Africa. In doing this he rendered a vast spiritual and psychological service to black people in this country.

The truth is that we can trace our spiritual ancestry better than we can trace our biological ancestry. Our biological ancestry may be diffused in the complexities of historical circumstance but our spiritual ancestry leaps vast expanses of time, history, and geography to the ancient land of Palestine.

I shall never forget the thrill of my first sight of the Holy Land. Marian and I were leading a tour group and we had been flying all night from New York to Tel Aviv. The majority of the people on the plane were Jews and many of them were Orthodox Jews. At daybreak Marian nudged me to consciousness and said, "Look behind you." As I glanced over my shoulder I saw several men standing facing the wall of the aircraft, praying their morning prayers. They were an awesome sight, with their long beards, black suits and hats on.

Later, a sense of excitement began to build in the airplane. It became apparent that we were approaching the coast of Israel. Suddenly a shout pierced the air and people began to clap their hands. Spontaneously they began to sing a Hebrew song:*"Havenu Shalom Aleichem"* (We bring peace to you.) The joy was electric. I looked out the window. The hair on the back of my neck rose and a chill went down my spine. There it was -- Israel! Suddenly I *knew* I was home!

As the week progressed, no amount of commercialization, no obscuring of the facts of the past hindered my feeling that *here* is where it all began for me! I stood at Mamre, now only an open field with an abandoned water cistern, and recalled the word of God to Abraham: "I will make of you a great nation; and I will bless you, and make your name great, so that you will be a blessing." (Genesis 12:2)

Abraham had come to Mamre, leaving the land of Ur of the Chaldees at the direction of God. Wherever his descendants have gone, God has been with them, from the wilderness of Sinai to the ovens of Auschwitz to the new nation of Israel. To have been chosen by God is their identity and their destiny.

The working out of the awareness of who God is has taken place in the consciousness of the Jews. When famine threatened the existence of Israel, they found their relief at the feet of Joseph in Egypt. When Egypt proved to be a long and devastating slavery, they found their freedom in Moses. When freedom became bitter and the desert of Sinai became a festering sore of complaint, they found God faithful. Hebrew ethics is not merely a response to the commanding voice of God. It is a slow and careful working out of the implications of a faithful response to the God who *has been faithful* to them. This was the covenant with Moses:

> Now therefore, if you will obey my voice
> and keep my covenant, you shall be my own
> possession among all the peoples; for all
> the earth is mine, and you shall be to me a
> kingdom of priests and a holy nation ....
> The people replied, "All that the Lord has
> spoken we will do." (Exodus 9:5-8)

The history of the Hebrews in the Old Testament is an undulating history of faithfulness and unfaithfulness.

Unfaithfulness was always marked by judgment and tragedy. But tragedy was always tempered with promise -- the
promise of God. Gradually a new awareness began to take
shape in the mind of the prophet Jeremiah:

> Behold, the days are coming, says the Lord,
> when I will make a new covenant with the
> house of Israel and the house of Judah, not
> like the covenant which I made with their
> fathers when I took them by the hand to
> bring them out of the land of Egypt, my
> covenant which they broke though I was their
> husband.... I will put my law within them
> and I will write it on their hearts and I will
> be their God and they will be my people.
>   (Jeremiah 31:31-33)

Nevertheless, Jeremiah's predicted judgment of God
came true. The tribes of Benjamin and Judah (the only
ones remaining of the twelve tribes of Israel) found themselves in exile in Babylon, Jerusalem destroyed. From
the lips of the prophet Isaiah came the word of the Lord:

> Comfort, comfort my people...
> Speak tenderly to Jerusalem,
> And cry to her that her warfare is ended,
> That her iniquity is pardoned.
>   (Isaiah 40:1, 2)

And then the awareness of a new act of God took fo-
cus in the mind of Isaiah:

> But you, Israel, my servant, Jacob, whom
> I have chosen... you whom I took from the
> ends of the earth.... I have given you as
> a covenant to the people, a light to the na-
> tions.   (Isaiah 41:8, 9; 42:6)

The purpose of God was to redeem the world, not
just Israel. The servant of God was not to be a self-serving

servant, nor even a self-righteous servant. He was to be
a serving servant.

When Jesus was hanging on the cross, he felt himself to be, or at least the early church felt him to be, the
faithful remnant of Israel reduced to *one!* This was at
least intimated in the upper room at the last supper. Jesus'
solemn mood was punctuated by the misunderstandings of
the disciples, the betrayal of Judas, and the bread and
wine. As Jesus took the cup, he gave thanks and said to
the disciples, "Drink of it, all of you, for this is my
blood of the covenant, which is poured out for many for
the forgiveness of sins." (Matthew 26:27)

Jesus had been desperately trying to prepare the
disciples and others for the task inherent in being chosen.
He instructs them to make love the mark of their alle-
giance to him. Then he reminds them, "You have not chosen me, but I have chosen you... that you should bear fruit
and that your fruit should abide." (John 15:16)

> Peter said it concisely:
> You are a chosen race, a royal priesthood,
> a holy nation, God's own people, that you
> may declare the wonderful deeds of Him
> who called you out of darkness into his
> marvelous light. Once you were no people,
> but now you are God's people; once you had
> not received mercy, but now you have re-
> ceived mercy. (I Peter 2:9, 10)

This is who we are and what we are about. This is
the reason for our relationship with other human beings.
We are those who have been chosen to bear fruit. And
Paul well knew what that fruit is. He said: "The fruit of
the Spirit is love, joy, peace, patience, kindness, goodness, faithfulness, gentleness, self-control."
(Galatians 5:22)

God has assured us that He will be with us to strengthen us in producing this fruit in the world. If we do this, the world will be a better place because we have been faithful.

12

LIVING TRUTH

You will know the truth, and the truth will make you free.

John 8:32

Two powerful images have been fermenting in my mind all week. Last Sunday night I began to picture Jesus confronting the Pharisees. They questioned his authority and accused him of bearing witness only to himself. The air was electric because Jesus was fully aware of their intent to kill him. The Pharisees were convinced that they were in possession of the truth about God. They were dedicated to seeing that the Jews were faithful to the claim of God. Their intensity was unparalleled. As for Jesus and the Pharisees, it was a standoff. Jesus' claim to be the truth was non-negotiable. When absolute claims to truth confront each other, somebody usually gets hurt.

The other image entered my mind on Monday morning. There it was on the front page of the Atlanta Constitution -- a large picture of men taking guns from the trunk of a car. This picture was taken in Greensboro, North

Carolina last November third. This was the shootout in which five members of the Communist Workers' Party were shot to death. It was a confrontation in which the participants also laid claim to a non-negotiable truth.

Those who were murdered had excellent academic credentials. Three were medical doctors, one of whom had a Harvard theology degree. One other was a *magna cum laude* graduate of Duke and the fifth person was the president of her student body. By contrast, the perpetrators were all high school dropouts struggling in their own morass of frustration and cultural oppression -- an oppression, ironically, which the ones who were killed wanted to help alleviate.

Here are the scenes: Jesus confronting Pharisees, each claiming ultimate truth, non-negotiable. Communists confronting Ku Klux Klan members and Nazis, each group claiming to be guided by an ultimate truth, non-negotiable.

When Jesus and the Pharisees were confronting each other in the Temple, they were not discussing mere matters of opinion. They were appealing to something ultimate -- the nature of truth. The fundamental question of humankind is whether there is any ultimate value which lays claim on everything else.

In our lifetime it is not simply a question whether truth will survive. It is a question whether *anything* is an ultimate value. On every hand we hear the assertion that truth is relative -- relative to changing cultures, changing situations, changing perceptions. The relativity of truth is so much a part of the consciousness of our society that a certain cynicism has become characteristic of even the well-informed schoolboy. He is not likely to be as cynical as Pontius Pilate. You remember that Pilate asked Jesus, "What *is* truth?" But our schoolboy *is* likely to want to know *whose* truth is at issue. We have come to the place in the propaganda struggle that the average American is about as skeptical of his own government's pronouncements as he is those of the Soviet Union.

The French critic, Vinet, once wrote, "Most friends of truth love it as Frederic the Great loved music. It used to be said of him that, strictly speaking, he was not fond of music, but of the flute, and not indeed fond of the flute, but of *his* flute." Mark Twain observed that he had never known a real seeker after truth. Sooner or later everyone engaged in the search found what he was looking for and gave up the quest. Much of the disillusionment with the church derives from this type of pattern. Karl Barth said, "The supreme sin of man is that even in his religion he is always twisting the truth to serve his own selfish ends and private ideas."

However accurate these observations may be, somehow persons seem to long for the survival of the kind of values which will call persons back to moral standards which will permit people to live in the world without total destruction or total chaos.

It is a matter of fact that persons have been relying upon the reality of truth from our earliest recorded history:

(1) This inscription was found on an ancient Egyptian temple: "God finds his satisfaction in truth."

(2) Confucius, whose wisdom became foundational for the Chinese way of life, said, "I do not know how a man is to get on without truthfulness."

(3) The Buddhist teaching says, "Hold fast to the truth as to a lamp."

(4) Mohammed wrote: "God speaks the truth."

If there is nothing ultimate, then there is nothing to keep humankind from returning to the jungle and finally to annihilation. However, the strange thing about the threatened death of truth in our time is that more people are claiming to be in possession of it than ever before in history. All continue to swear by it, thousands die for it, and most of us seem to want it on our side.

I believe that human survival depends upon those values which make civilization possible, which make morality necessary, and which bring persons under the control of a reality greater than themselves. This means that truth *must* live and we must help it live. We must stop this insistence upon "our truth" as a possession, whether we be a nation, a religious group, or a political party. We need to catch again the exultant spirit of Euripides, who said, "When once I had seen the truth, there was no drug I could take to unsee it, and lose again what I had seen."

Nevertheless, we must avoid the kind of tunnel vision which permits us to see only what others want us to see, whether those others be media people, political people, or religious people. We need to develop the capacity to make distinctions about kinds of truth without denying whatever validity each kind may have.

We can distinguish three kinds of truth expressing themselves in the world.

THERE IS TRUTH WHICH LIVES BY ITS WHOLENESS.

This is truth of fact. A fact is just there. One may deny it, but it remains to sit in judgment upon the denial. Albert Camus expressed it well when he said, "Facts are facts, and whoever says the sky is blue when it is gray is prostituting words and preparing the way for tyranny. "We *have* to have consistency in descriptive language.

Truth of fact is the darling of the scientist -- as it ought to be. Scientific method as a means of finding and establishing facts and verifying hypotheses is a boon to humankind. Truth which lives by its wholeness *coheres.* It makes sense. It provides a structure by which one can evaluate his/her own reasoning powers. This truth transcends ideologies, nations, and planets.

THERE IS THE TRUTH WHICH LIVES BY ITS WITS.

We understand this way of thinking very well. It says, "Let's be practical," or "That's the way the world is." This is the characteristic stance of the American people in particular. We have been conditioned to be practical in our actions and pragmatic in our thinking. Pragmatism has been called the only distinctive American philosophy. That is the point of view which says, "If it works it has value." This became a powerful part of the educational training of generations of American children.

This view has been twisted out of shape in our time. It is almost a fact that "You can't fight city hall," but not quite. It is almost a fact that "You have to go along with the crowd," but not quite. It is almost a fact that "One has to be a little crooked to get along in business," but not quite. Commonly accepted practice can be the road to the demoralization of society. However admirable may be the desire to test every idea and every value by the question, "How well does it work?" the result of that approach was a perversion of its own ideal into a self-destructing reality.

This self-destructive tendency can be seen in many places. It is vividly illustrated in Tom, a character in the novel, *The Man In The Grey Flannel Suit.* Tom is a businessman. He wants to help the man for whom he works, but he struggles with the question of how honest he can afford to be with his employer. "After all," he thinks, "I am being paid to do what the boss wants me to do. If I disagree with him all the time, he may decide that he doesn't need me." Tom decided to play the game and go through the motions until he becomes "big enough to be honest without being hurt." Nevertheless, Tom realizes the irony of his situation. He concludes, "How smoothly one becomes, not a cheat, exactly, nor really a liar, just a man who'll say anything for pay."

No, the truth which lives by its wits outwits itself!

THERE IS THE TRUTH WHICH LIVES BY ITS WITNESS.

I believe the truth which lives by its witness can redeem the truth of fact from the so-called truth which lives by its wits. We must not drift into a pattern of using our technology in destructive ways.

William Penn lamented on one occasion that truth suffers more from the heat of its defenders than from the arguments of its opposers. We need to come to the place at which the defenders of truth are not propagandists (not even church propagandists), nor soldiers, nor witchhunters, but *servants*. Truth which lives by its witness suffers damage when that witness is weak or timid or hypocritical.

The truth of the Christian faith is so personal in nature that the Christian who says he loves Christ and then denies him by his actions does damage to the whole cause. The person who says (by professing Christ and joining the church) that the worship of God and the service of God are the highest values of life but who does not worship and who does not serve -- that person strikes a blow against the truth of God. The world will simply not listen to a church which has made its witness a farce and its faith a fraud.

Nevertheless, the world *will* listen to truth which has come alive in service and sacrifice. The world will listen to an Albert Schweitzer. Here was a man whose brilliant mind and deep piety were combined with a magnificent capacity to sense the rare beauties of majestic music. Schweitzer's academic life was crowned with four doctor's degrees. His contributions in theology and music set him apart as one of the giants of his generation. Yet, at the height of his powers he abandoned the arena of public affairs and went into the jungles of Africa to serve the natives as a medical doctor. The audacity of such an overwhelming undertaking has only been matched by the intensity of his devotion to one gripping truth: "reverence for life." When one lives his/her truth in such a way as that, the world takes notice.

But the world also takes notice when five Communists are murdered by a group of prejudiced and culturally deprived Ku Klux Klansmen. When people give their lives for a cause, even unintentionally, it makes its impact. What, then, is to be done to clarify the distinction between those who die for a cause and those whose cause adds to the value of life? What is the difference?

The difference is in the long view. We know what value is even when we cannot put it to a test tube. Jesus Christ has stood the test of time. His truth rings true in life. In him we see how life *ought* to be lived. Christ is the standard by which the Klan and the Communist are judged and found wanting. When you live in Christ life takes on its fullest meaning. You can teach this truth to your children -- but you have to *live* it.

13

OVERCOMING DOUBT

*Thomas...said.... "unless I see...I will
not believe."*   *John 20:24ff*

*Peter got out of the boat and walked on
the water and came to Jesus; but when he saw
the wind, he was afraid, and beginning to sink
he cried out, "Lord, save me."*
                    Matthew 14:29,30

I don't like snakes. There is a reason. One day
when I was about eight years of age I was walking down a
path toward the railroad tracks. It was a stony, red clay
path. It was summertime and I was barefoot. I was pay-
ing too much attention to the stones which were hurting my
feet and not enough attention to the path. Suddenly I realized that my next step would put me right on top of a coiled
orange and black snake. I froze with fear and then leaped
for a world record! I was a half-mile down the road before I stopped running.

When I excitedly reported this event to my parents,
they asked me whether it was a black snake with orange
rings or an orange snake with black rings! There are people who notice such things, but I am not one of them. They
patiently explained to me that one is a harmless and beneficial snake and the other is deadly poisonous. The

93

distinction between poisonous and non-poisonous snakes is an important one to know. But to tell you the truth, my strategy is to leave them *all* alone!

Some people treat their doubts as I treat snakes. They make no distinctions and try to stay away from all of them. The trouble with that is the doubts won't go away. They cannot be effectively dealt with in that fashion. Doubt can strike fear into the half-informed and half-believing heart. It can coil menacingly about the brain and strike poison into the soul. It can immobilize with anxiety and leave cold sweat popping on the forehead. It can slither through the grass of one's perceptions as a menacing, almost unconscious presence. Like the fangs of a rattler, it can tear away the assumptions of childhood with a devastating ferocity.

We can run away from a snake but we cannot run away from our doubts. Once we are conscious of them, they tend to become bigger and bigger until they are dealt with. We can fence out a snake, but we will discover that fencing out our doubts is the same as enclosing our own minds in a cage. *We* become the prisoner. It is crucial that we learn to distinguish poisonous from non-poisonous doubts. These incidents in our scripture can help us. They vividly depict the vastly different kinds of doubt and suggest ways of dealing with them.

1. Thomas faced a doubt in the head (intellectual doubt). He could not believe what was inconceivable to him. Thomas could only believe when he was convinced by observable facts. His faith could only be sustained when his doubts were dead.

Most of us struggle from time to time with ideas or viewpoints which are inconceivable to us. We worry about that. It should prove helpful to realize that this kind of doubt is not necessarily poisonous. Intellectual doubt is one facet of the thinking process. In this sense, a person who says, "I have no doubts" is merely announcing that he/she has stopped thinking. This kind of doubt only becomes a problem when it is directed against ideas that are fondly cherished.

The question of truth is very much at issue in a world of competing religious points of view, a climate in which it is required that all claims to truth fall under the methods of the laboratory sciences, and a general assumption that the world is self-explanatory. Thus, our present human situation is a doubt producing situation. Many of our fondly cherished beliefs are threatened. The question we need to ask ourselves is whether God stands or falls by *our* cherished beliefs.

Jesus' treatment of Thomas would suggest that intellectual questions are legitimate. He did not condemn Thomas because he could not believe. Jesus said, "Reach forth your hand and place it in my side, and be not faithless but believing." Thomas' faith had been crushed by the shocking realities of the crucifixion. Thomas became a believer again when external evidence convinced him. Unfortunately the tide of time has swept us beyond those external evidences. But that does not mean that our minds have to stop working, or that we have to "park our brains to save our souls."

On the contrary, Jesus gives every indication that intellectual questions are honored. A second-rate thought process does not do credit to the God of truth. Even so, it is important to keep in mind that this is only one kind of doubt, and the way to deal with this kind of doubt is to *use* it creatively. In intellectual doubt the process is to meet doubt producing situations by doubting them. That is, keep pressing every question until the truth emerges. To the intellectual doubter the best advice is," *keep on growing.*'

2. On the other hand Peter faced a different kind of doubt. His was a doubt in the soul. This is the kind of situation which scares a person out of his/her wits, the doubt in which one's destiny is at stake (existential doubt).

Not like Thomas, who put external evidences ahead of a supportive faith, Peter was faced with a sinking situation. Carl Michalson suggested that Jesus named Peter "the Rock" not because of his foundational qualities but for his sinking qualities. Peter's doubt did not destroy his faith, it *produced* his faith! When Peter was sinking he turned his full trust toward the face of his Lord. He said, "Lord, save me!" Peter was no coward. But he would not trust anything that would not hold him up. When he was sinking, he did not turn to swimming. He turned to *trusting*. Peter knew from experience with Jesus a simple fact we seem to overlook, and that is that we have no buoyancy within ourselves.

Doubt in the soul can give you more than a sinking feeling. It can mean death. Of course, to die is not necessarily the worst experience of a human being. The *worst* experience is to doubt the reasons for living in such a way that life itself becomes utterly meaningless.

Doubt of the soul can only be overcome by a direct trusting relationship with the Lord. Jesus would not want any of us to stop short of a faith which will support us. This is not the place for intellectual games, nor even conceptualization problems. When you are sinking it is time to trust the Lord. For this kind of doubt, trust burns away the clouds of doubt like the morning sun burns away the fog of the dawn.

For these two thousand years trusting Jesus has lifted many a person out of the sinking bog of despair onto the sound rock of a secure relationship with God. Trusting Christ works! What doesn't work is half-trusting him.

This is not an intellectual problem. This is a soul problem. People who have learned to trust Christ have usually discovered that many intellectual problems recede into the background. If they do not dissipate entirely, at least they become secondary considerations in the light of the secure relationship with God which they enjoy. To the existential doubter the best advice is, *"keep on trusting."*

3. But what about the doubt that does not result from the inadequacy of one's beliefs, or even from threatening circumstances? There is a kind of doubt which seems to derive from the need to be a doubter (pathological doubt). This is the doubt which emanates not from the top of the head but from the bottom of the heart. This kind of doubt cannot be overcome with facts and assurances. It does no good to tell such a person to "have faith."

John Dewey once observed that, "a personal doubt is pathological unless it is a reflection of a situation which is problematic." In simpler terms, that seems to mean that if you are not about to step on a *real* snake, don't create one! Yet people *do* create doubts, even when the intellectual situation or the circumstantial situation does not require it.

We know about personality types who hold their beliefs fanatically, not necessarily because their beliefs are good ones, but because they are the kind of person who can never be wrong. We know about people who hold their beliefs so loosely that they can agree with whatever point of view they encounter.

We also know doubters who will never be convinced with facts and who never give the Lord a chance in their lives. This is the person who is too proud to believe. He can surrender himself to no one. This is the person for whom trusting God is a sign of weakness. On the other hand, we know persons who are too humble to believe.

They cannot accept the fact that God loves them. Thus, they refuse faith as an option for their lives.

This kind of doubt cannot be solved with intellectual answers. Neither does it do any good to tell such a person to have faith. Faith does have the power to wilt pride and to overcome inordinate humility. But faith cannot be tried on like a new suit of clothes. Faith comes by the power of God into the life of the doubter in a somewhat analogous way as good humor comes by the power of a good joke into the life of a grouch. When you tell a grouch the right story, the story itself arouses him to good humor. If it does not, you do not tell him that you have told him a joke. You keep trying to find the right story. It doesn't do any good to tell a grouch to cheer up.

Emotionally based doubt is only resolved by undercutting the need for the doubt. This is what the Gospel does when it tells us who we are as children of God. To know that we belong to God, that God loves us and calls us to reflect his presence in our lives, carries with it the power to dissipate doubt. We don't have to argue people into the Kingdom of God. Neither do we need to keep telling people to have faith. We *do* have to keep telling them who they are as children of God, even when they do not believe in God. For the word of God carries its own inexplicable power to transform life.

Mark Twain once said, "The difference between the right word and almost the right word is the difference between lightning and the lightning bug." God has given us the right word in Jesus Christ, and faith comes by hearing the word of God. When God strikes you, he will make a difference in your life. So to the emotional doubter the best advice is, *"keep on listening."*

14

FAITH

(God) said, "Take your son, your only son
Isaac, whom you love, and go into the land of
Moriah, and offer him there as a burnt offering....
                                        Genesis 22:2

The Associated Press reported that on July 6, 1922 John Shell died in Kentucky at the age of one hundred and thirty-four years, and that he left two children -- one ninety and the other *seven* years old!

If you think that is funny it is nothing to the side-splitting laughter of Abraham when God told him that he would give him a son by Sarah. Abraham laughed and rolled on the ground. He said to himself, "Shall a child be born to a man who is a hundred years old? Shall Sarah, who is ninety years old, bear a child? (Genesis 17:17)

God's covenant with Abraham is recorded in the twelfth chapter of Genesis. In keeping that covenant Abraham became the spiritual father of the Hebrew and the Christian people. We trace our heritage of faith to Abraham. The one characteristic phrase which rings across

99

the centuries in our history is this: "Abraham believed God, and it was reckoned to him as righteousness." (Genesis 15:6)

This was the key phrase for the Hebrew community. They interpreted faith to mean obedience. So do we. The contemporary theologian Emil Brunner says, "Faith is obedience -- nothing else." This is the key to the nature of faith as Paul understood it. St. Augustine and Martin Luther are two other epochal figures in the Church who emphasized this understanding of faith. "Abraham believed God, and it was reckoned to him as righteousness."

This is not to relegate human conduct to a secondary role. On the contrary, it is to say that all our doings properly proceed from our basic commitment to God. All the fruits of moral conduct and generosity flow from an act of surrender so complete, so absolute, as to be overwhelming.

I was visiting with my mother this week. She is quite elderly and in a weakened condition. Yet she never fails to ask about our church. She said, "How many people are being saved?" I thought for a moment, because I knew what she meant. Then I said, "Well, I do not know. We have a good many people joining the church, some on the profession of their faith." That was not a full answer, really. How many *are* being saved? I trust that all of us are being saved, but I am not very confident of that because I suspect that a considerable number of us are not surrendered to God. We are playing games with our faith and are only partially -- very partially! -- trusting in him. Let us mark it well, salvation means trusting God with our lives and being surrendered to him in our priorities.

Paul Tillich is talking about priorities when he speaks of faith as ultimate concern. Faith is a passion of the spirit of a person who is ultimately concerned about his/

her life and destiny and what that destiny means. One
takes upon himself the risk of believing God. This is why
Tillich says that doubt is not a lack of faith. Doubt is not
against faith. Doubt is an element of faith. There is no
faith without the tension of the risk of believing the impossible.

> *The tension*
> *of the risk*
> *of believing*
> *the impossible!*

Every person of faith *has* faith and takes the step of
surrender in spite of doubt. The appropriate polarity is
faith on the one hand and *indifference* on the other. Indifference, not doubt, is the opposite of faith. This is why
Soren Kierkegaard, a Danish philosopher of one hundred
years ago who has influenced so many in our time, has
said, "Faith is a leap." Faith includes belief, but it is an
act of trust. To believe God is to trust him. To trust him
is to be obedient to his will insofar as one can discern it.

To understand faith is vastly different from being
able to have faith. This is due to the nature of our human
situation, which is vividly characterized by Friedrich
Nietzsche. He said, "Man is a rope stretched over an
abyss." Human existence is today being characterized in
Nietzsche's terms. Ours is a tremendously insecure
world -- and the abyss is deep! We are not merely threatened by our own individual finitude. We are threatened
with *extinction!*

Faced with this insecure situation, we can try to
hold on to both ends of the rope. We can try to establish
our security in the business we develop, the friends we
have or the money we accumulate. We can feverishly hold
on to those things we see and feel. We can ride out the
situation in a frenetic sequence of pleasure-events.

Or we can trust God. Abraham believed God, and it was considered sufficient. Is that an incredibly naive stance? It *is* certainly incredibly complex, for believing God involves being obedient to his will. It *is* certainly incredibly difficult, for it reaches beyond the scope of human intellect. This may explain why Kierkegaard said, "There is no way to understand the man of faith."

Abraham dared to believe the word of God when he said:

> As for Sarai your wife, you shall not call
> her Sarai, but Sarah shall be her name. I
> will bless her, and moreover I will give
> you a son by her; I will bless her and she
> shall be a mother of nations; kings of
> peoples shall come from her. (Genesis 17:15,16)

In this, the *tension* of the *risk* of *believing* the *impossible* reached its critical point. *This* was ridiculous! Keep in mind that Abraham was already a man of faithfulness. He was a good man by his best lights. He was already fulfilling the law of the tithe. Material decisions did not keep him away from God. But after all, there *has* to be a limit! Nevertheless, Abraham believed God.

Only when Abraham plunged beyond the boundaries of the incredible did God send him Isaac -- bone of his bone and flesh of his flesh. More than his pride and joy, Isaac was ultimate --Isaac was living proof of the faithfulness of God. Every time Abraham saw little Isaac he knew God was trustworthy.

Everything was going well for Abraham in his old age. His wealth was established; his future was secure; his child was thriving. One day God said to him, "Take your son, your only son Isaac, whom you love, and go to the land of Moriah, and offer him there as a burnt offering upon one of the mountains of which I shall tell you." (Genesis 22:2)

I can imagine Abraham's response: "Offer Isaac? Surely I have misunderstood you! You gave him to me. He is the sign of your promise to me!"

"Offer Isaac!"

Oh, how that command rings in my ears! What is the most important thing in the world to you? "Offer Isaac!" How can one understand the meaning of sacrifice? "Offer Isaac!" What is the nature of faith? "Offer Isaac!"

We have reached the ultimate limit of our understanding: to offer Isaac is *murder*, not sacrifice.

God is first or he is not God. It will simply not do to toy with the alternatives. What is the will of God for my life? Whatever else it may mean, it means *total surrender* to him.

Having reached the upper limits, it remains for each of us to fill in the rest of it. How many of us are being saved? We are all being called to identify our Isaac and understand the meaning of sacrifice.

15

THE LOGIC OF FAITH

*I know your works. You are neither cold
nor hot. Would that you were cold or hot!*
Revelation 3:15

"Be reasonable!" Isn't that what you tell your wife
when she is being unreasonable? Have you ever heard a
woman tell a man, "Be reasonable?" I don't recall it.
Marian has never suggested that I be reasonable. I have
always been reasonable! It is she who is not reasonable!

There is something to that. Psychologists tell us
that women have a tendency to speak more from their emo-
tions, more from that depth of sensitivity which broadens
the scope of analysis. And we find ourselves getting into
difficulty because we relate to different persons on different wave lengths.

The problem of relating the rational to the nonration-
al (which is also valid, and sometimes more valid than the
rational) has been our problem in this century perhaps
more than any other. We are the century of the practically

reasonable. We are characterized in this century by the technological application of reason. We apply the working of the mind in terms of common sense and in terms of experimental research. We have made that the standard for truth and conceptualization.

We are reasonable people. That is both our bane and our blessing. The fact that we are reasonable often frustrates us in our Christian faith. We find ourselves trying to plumb the depths of realities which transcend reason. We find ourselves trying to believe things which our minds reject as inconceivable (as though that is the basis of our faith). We struggle with that. We are hung on the horns of this dilemma -- between reason and faith.

I want to suggest to you that those are not irreconcilable opposites. It is not necessary to be hung there. Our problem as Christians is *not* that we are so reasonable about our faith, but rather that we do not follow the logic of our faith. Logic is, after all, the instrument of reason.

The main instrument of logic is the syllogism. It is a three- step process by which reasoning is evaluated and kept consistent. Logical thinking is the process of moving from one fact to another and then to a conclusion. For example, if the statement, "All men grow whiskers" is true; and the statement "I am a man" is true; then it follows necessarily that I grow whiskers. The third truth is embodied in the first two truths.

Most of us are not trained in the use of the syllogism, but we are conditioned by our culture to believe what "makes sense" to us. If something does not "make sense" to us, we either reject it or circumvent it in some way.

Christianity is on very insecure ground if it is based on an attempt to "get around" matters and ideas which it

cannot accept or communicate. Neither are we on very
secure ground when we are not as consistent in our *application* of our belief as we pride ourselves in being.

What I want to insist upon is that we follow *more precisely* the logic of our faith.

For example, if it is true that there be a god, and if
that god is like Jesus, then it follows... If it is *true* that
there be a god, and if that god be like Jesus, then it follows...

First, the logic of our belief in God is *faithfulness*.
Jesus pointed to the irony of it all when he said, "Why do
you call me Lord, Lord, and do not do what I tell you?"
If God is God, and if God is *ultimate* then what we have
come to understand about the nature of God is in the very
nature of a *necessity*, a command of our being in relationship to him.

Therefore, the opposite of faith in our Christian understanding is not reason. The opposite of faith is *indifference*. Fyodor Dostoyevsky in his novel, *The Possessed*,
had the monk Tikhon to say:

> Complete atheism is more respectable than
> worldly indifference.... A complete atheist
> stands on the last rung but one before abso-
> lute faith (he may or may not step higher),
> but an indifferent man has no faith at all,
> nothing but an ugly fear, and that only on
> rare occasions, if he is a sentimental man.

This is the clear meaning of the word of God to the
church at Laodicea. God abhors indifference more than
he abhors outright atheism. Once the truth about God is
seen, or at least sensed, then the necessities springing
from that relationship are clear.

Over the years I have been surprised as I have tried to express as clearly as I could the truth of the implications of the Gospel for a congregation of people who had stated in word and deed that they were followers of the Lord Jesus Christ, only to have someone say to me, "I admire your courage." There seems to have been an underlying assumption that the preacher should be sensitive to what the people may want to hear rather than the application of the Gospel to our human situation.

It is not courage to share with the Lord's people the best understanding one has of what the Lord's will is. That is logic! If God be God, and if God be like Jesus, it is incumbent upon us to be sensitive to his will and not our own. The logic of belief is faithfulness.

This explains Jesus' different expectations of the Romans, the Pharisees, and his disciples. Whereas he knew that the Romans would do the expedient thing, there is every indication that he expected more from the Pharisees, who, after all, had proclaimed that they wanted to do God's will. His disillusionment in the face of their betrayal may account for the ferocity of his denunciations of the scribes and Pharisees.

Jesus expected an entirely different relationship from his disciples than from those who followed him looking for bread, or healing, or a spectacle. Jesus does not want just so much of our time or our possessions. He says, "I want you!" The disciple of Jesus has renounced all his or her claims. He/she does not need to be petted or pampered. He/she has removed his/her feelings from his/her sleeves. He/she has denied his/her right to laziness, negative thinking, or foot dragging. The Christian *looks* for something to do, not for a way to do less.

Secondly, the logic of our *awareness* of the God who has revealed himself in Jesus is *gratitude*. The vital memory of the crucifixion is an awareness of the consummate self-giving of God. God loved the world so much that he gave his only son, that whoever believes in him should have eternal life. We are not the givers in this relationship. We are the receivers! We are the responders! Everything we do is a response to God's love, God's generosity.

If that response is a fountain of gratitude, the whole situation changes. One does not worship God out of a sense of duty, or social conformity. We do not give because other people are looking. We do not even give because the need is there. We give in a response to the superabundant generosity of God.

When Jesus told the story of the Pharisee and the publican he described the Pharisee as one who was aware only of himself. His sense of gratitude was warped. Of course, there is a strong element of truth in the Pharisee's perception. He said, "I thank thee that I am not as other men are." He was different. And by his lights he was better -- certainly better off. The Pharisee was condemned because he lost sight of the *source* of his blessing.

Finally, I want to suggest to you that the logic of our discipleship is *service*. We do not always seem to understand that simple fact. A Christian congregation (including the clergy, to be sure) is a complex of myriad motivations. Jesus understands that fact about us just as surely as he understood it about his disciples on the way to Jerusalem.

When Jesus was moving toward Jerusalem, and those who had been with him for instruction, who had seen his power, who had been awed by the magnificence of his ministry, overwhelmed by his sensitivity to the presence of almighty God in and through him, who were attuned to the Kingdom of God as well as they could be attuned to it, were with him. What were they doing? They were arguing over who would be the greatest! Who was going to sit at the right hand of the Lord in his glory!

Of course, this is in a congregation also. We have ego problems, sensitivity problems, who is going to be this, who is going to be consulted about that.

Jesus settled that issue, for then and now. Amidst that undercurrent of ambition, he stripped naked, wrapped himself in a towel and knelt before the leader of them all, Simon Peter, to wash his feet! Peter was appalled. He said, "Lord, you must not wash my feet!" Jesus replied, "Unless I wash your feet you can have no part of me." Simon then said, "Lord, then wash all of me!" Jesus said, "There is no need for me to wash all of you. I have given you an example, that you should do as I have done to you." (John 13:4ff)

Jesus was saying, "This is the way I am -- and this is the way our heavenly father wants you to be." In the most powerful and poignant way possible, Jesus turned our minds away from hierarchies and prerogatives and feelings of importance and said, "If you are my disciple you will look for ways to serve." That is what this congregation exists to do. We do not exist to see how little we can do for our Lord. We do not exist to place all our self-serving priorities first. We exist to search for *more* and *more* and *more* ways to serve! I think *that* is the logic of our faith.

Let's be reasonable!

16

PLEASURE WANTS ETERNITY

·... that they should seek God in the hope
that they might feel after him and find him.
                                    Acts 17:27

The Christian Gospel spread like wildfire throughout the Roman world. It was born in the marketplace and
it thrived in the world of ideas. The Apostle Paul was the
foremost carrier of the message of Christ, and he never
backed away from a debate. St. Paul, of all people, was
confident that the message of Christ could stand the test
of truth.

Why is it, then, that today it appears that college
students seem to move away from Christianity precisely
at the time when they are plunged most deeply into the
realm of ideas? Why does the general level of preaching
seem to be so innocuous?

To be a college student today can be a frightening
experience. Exhilarating, yes, but also frightening. College is the place where one encounters significant numbers

of persons who know vastly more than you do. It can be overwhelming to be made to feel that your intellectual assumptions, your moral judgments, your value systems, your clothes, your personality -- practically everything about you is *wrong*. Peer group pressures, sophisticated assumptions and presumptions can be stifling. Practically any professor who wants to do so can tear you apart, intellectually and emotionally. Whether he/she puts you together again is a matter of his/her own choice. That can be devastating!

Parents can not prepare you for this. High school rarely helps. The slight preparation the Church gives can appear almost a betrayal. A college student may have some reason for bitterness, considering the appalling lack of preparation his church gives him/her to face the world of ideas.

All I can say at this point is: "Don't give up!" The Church has been at the center of the struggle of ideas since its beginning. Our present-day failure is more of a sign of the times than an indication that Christianity cannot measure up. Preachers who fail to deal with the difficult ideas may have fallen victim to the suspicion that their congregations do not want to struggle with hard problems. Hence your most popular expressions of Protestant Christianity in this country are either a naive easy-answer biblicism or a success-oriented form of positive thinking.

St. Paul addressed himself to the intellectuals in Athens and drew their attention away from their generalized search for something new and interesting. He focused their attention upon God who "made the world and everything in it," the God who revealed himself in Jesus and expressed himself in the power of the resurrection. This is the God who placed within the minds of persons an inveterate desire that "they should seek God, in the hope that they might feel after him and find him."

From the beginning Christianity has been based on the premise that persons are called to be fully human in a broken world. What does it mean in the twentiety century to say that one is "called?" What does it mean to say that one is "human?" What does it mean to say that the world is "broken?"

When Augustine of Hippo was converted to Christ in the fourth century, he thought of himself as "called." He wrote, "Thou hast made us for thyself, O God, and our hearts are restless until they find their rest in thee." This expression rings a bell in the minds of most Christians in the sense that we also come to the conclusion that we have been created for God's purposes in the world.

Nevertheless, such an assertion makes no sense at all to vast numbers of people in our society and in the rest of the world. These people no longer act out of the center of Christian belief. They make no effort to justify themselves in terms of Christian morality. They do not express the meaning of life in terms of Christian responsibility. Morality is viewed as a mere matter of opinion. They are simply not on the Christian wave length.

Is it possible for the concept of being called to have any meaning for persons such as these? Yes, because there is one common bond among us -- so-called modern man's predicament. Many of the contemporary analysts of the human situation agree that modern man is sick: alienated, frustrated, neurotic, empty and in despair. We find ourselves in a world in which the problems boggle the mind and frustrate our spirits. I am suggesting that modern man's sickness may very well be a form of homesickness, in which our longing for God rises above not merely our problems but above every attempt at a solution to our problems. This is at least something of what it means to be called -- that our very emptiness and restlessness become an indication of a lost destiny.

What does it mean to say that our world is "broken?" It is not simply that the world is divided into competing ideologies. It is more like saying that the world has come apart at the seams.

When the contemporary artist views the world, it becomes "without form and void." Blurred forms and shades of color are "suggestive" of inner states and moods of the artist. Dean Samuel Miller of the Harvard Divinity School tells of seeing an exhibit in the New York Museum of Modern Art titled "The Images of Man." He later discussed it with Paul Tillich. Tillich said, "Wasn't it a nightmare?" Miller agreed that it was. And then he asks, "Why does a capable artist like Giacometti make man so tall and thin, like an insect? Why does Cessanne go to some junk heap and pick up a lot of pieces of iron and cinders from a furnace and put them together and call this the form of a man? And why does Oliviera, the Italian, portray humans with no face — no face — moving through an empty fog of a world?" All this reminds Miller of Picasso, who portrays man with nose, mouth, and ears, but they are all out of place and out of proportion. The human being is seen as distorted, perverted, broken. Berdyaev, the Russian philosopher, saw it all coming when he asked, "Will the creature who inherits the world still be worthy of the name 'man'?"

Some philosophers are beginning to ask whether everything is not "pseudo" or false, whether everything is not, at best, only a useful lie — and thus whether at the end of every ideology there is nothing but nothingness. This is what we mean by "brokenness." It is the end of the line. This is an attitude in which one no longer says "No" to meaning. The question of meaning is just not allowed to appear. Everything becomes a matter of unquestioned surrender to the moment, to the immediate activity, the immediate duty, the immediate pleasure. It is a refusal to see one's life in terms of any purpose or meaning beyond the given moment. This perception led the sensitive genius, Friedrich Nietzsche, to declare that God is dead, by which he meant that all meaning, all value had evaporated.

Nietzsche saw the problem, but he also saw the solution. He said, "Pleasure wants eternity, deep, deep eternity." It was precisely this sense of eternity that Nietzsche could not find.

St. Paul knew, and I hope each one of us will discover, that Jesus Christ is the way God uses to lead persons to himself. The hunger for something more than pleasure or power or peer acceptance may well be a hunger for God.

Many college students seem to lose sight of this inveterate hunger for something more. I think it is due to the fact that college confronts one with a massive amount of information and variety of viewpoints. This causes many persons to conclude that Christianity must be rather weak by comparison.

Who can help but admire the courage of the existentialist, who finds it very troublesome that God does not exist and proceeds bravely to face a world in which children suffer and die? He defines humanity by his own act of existing. He invents his values in the laboratory of human experience. That approach sounds like one a brave and practical person might make.

Who can help but admire the optimism of the humanist, who finds no reason to assume more than that human life is the ultimate value? He sees no reason to seek shelter from his cosmic loneliness in the arms of some divinized father-figure. He regards the move to divine authority as an act of cowardice -- a failure to assume responsibility for one's world. The dedication which is needed is a dedication to human progress by human effort. Technology is the instrument by which humans can make a better world for everybody.

I want to ask you young people to take a good, long look at these alternatives. But I also want you to ask yourselves whether such optimism is anything more than a positive form of despair. You will be re-reading Orwell's *Nineteen Eighty-Four* in the next year or two. I want you to see what "utopian" optimism can be without the guiding hand of God.

I submit that both the courage of the existentialist and the optimism of the humanist are not less an assumption than each of them charges the Christian understanding to be. I suggest to you that the preoccupation of these people is an indication of the search for God -- for the ultimate value which St. Paul described to the people of Athens.

The college scene is an exciting place to be. But please make sure that you learn enough of the history of ideas to discern when people who claim to deny God pull Christian concepts out from under the rug of Western culture and put their own brand upon them as though they are new ideas.

What we desire is to be human in the fullest sense of the word. We want to know who we are and what our vocation is in the world. Only as our sickness is properly diagnosed will it be possible to recover some degree of health amidst the brokenness of our world.

Therefore we define our sickness as homesickness -- as an emptiness which is caused by separation from the source of our existence. We see meaning in the Christian concept of responsibility to God. Man is not absolute but relative. We are relative to our creator, who lets us

know who we are and what is our vocation in the world.
We are in the world because we were *placed* here. Our
existence is relative to the ground of our being whom we
call God. We were created in the image of God. That is
our vocation -- to image or reflect the reality of God. We
see our identity historically focused in that people who
have engaged themselves in responding to the understanding of existence precipitated in their history by events in
which they see the meaningfulness of God's purpose.

From these events and their subsequent interpreta-
tions has come an understanding of man as a trustee and a
steward over the events of the world. Man is responsible
for his world. But he is *responsible to God the Creator*.
This relieves him of no decisions. Rather, it heightens
the significance of those decisions. The Christian has not
found an escape from the world. He has been called to an
acute responsibility for the world. God is not the One to
whom man escapes. He is the One to whom man *answers*.

Therefore, it is not sufficient to say that twentieth
century man's loneliness is only apparent (as with Huxley)
or that his illness is inevitable (as with Sartre). We must
say that man has been human before and he longs to be
human again, even in a broken world. It is not that the
decisions are difficult and the world is hard. The world
has always been hard, and that is a relatively insignificant
matter. As Nietzsche said, "He who has a *why* to live can
endure any *how*."

The Christian is saying that man defines himself in
the context of his relation with God -- which relation can
only be defined by God himself as he meets us in his word.
In the Judeo-Christian history the Christian locates himself in the world -- he finds his identity. But this is a history
with a broadening scope and a redemptive purpose. Thus he
finds his vocation, his values, his tasks, and his satisfactions -- satisfactions which have about them the aura of "deep,
deep, eternity."

17

SAVE THE CHILDREN

(Jesus) said to them, "Let the children
come to me, do not hinder them; for to such
belongs the kingdom of God."

Mark 10:14

The more famous a person becomes, the more
people there seem to be gathered around him/her telling
everyone how busy he/she is. Jesus experienced that --
to his great irritation! The disciples whom he had gathered
to help him had become his "protectors." This scripture
reflects a typical scene toward the end of Jesus' ministry.
He had become famous. Throngs of people pressed in
upon him. Scribes and Pharisees wanted to discuss the
Law. Others wanted a judgment between disputing parties.
Many wanted to be healed. Their persistence was almost
overwhelming. Presumably the disciples were justified in
turning the children away from Jesus. "Too busy! Too
busy!" is a frustrating echo in the midst of pressing need.
We have all experienced that. The busier we become, the
more the priorities have to be carefully established. Jesus
made it clear that, for him, the chief priority was the
children. Incidentally, this is one of the few times we see

him angry. When children are being hindered from the blessing of God, it is *time* to be angry.

Jesus said, "Let the children come to me, and do not hinder them." On another occasion he said, "He who hinders a child, it would be better for him to have a millstone hung around his neck and he be drowned in the depths of the sea." (Mark 9:42) The message from God is clear: "Do not ruin the children." Jesus knew, and we are beginning to realize, that a society is judged by what happens to its children.

Periodically we are reminded of how tenuous the situation is with our children. My sharpest reminder came from seeing the movie version of William Golding's *Lord of the Flies*. A group of children had been stranded on an island. At first their civilized rationality prevailed. They shrank from killing anything and ate only fruit. It occurred to them that they should be prepared to defend themselves, so they sharpened their walking sticks. Then they began to use the sticks to kill for food. One day they had killed a pig. They became intrigued with the blood of the animal and playfully began to decorate their faces. As they were exploring the island they discovered the fully clothed corpse of an airplane pilot hanging from a tree by his parachute straps. As they saw this image in the semi-darkness fear began to consume them. They put the head of the pig on a stick in sacrifice to the "monster."

A struggle developed among the children between the forces of rationality and morality on the one hand and superstition, fear, power, and conformity on the other. The larger boys began to oppress the smaller ones. They nicknamed one boy "Piggy" because he was fat and wore thick glasses. They stole his glasses as a "joke" and Piggy had to wander around half blind. They built a "fortress" on the side of the mountain in order to defend themselves from the "monster." Their orgies of fear and excitement increased. One of the smaller boys came running to tell them that the "monster" was merely a corpse. As he came through the woods they shouted, "It's the monster! It's the monster! Kill him!" And they killed him with their sticks.

Afterward, one boy was trying to tell the others that what they had done was murder. Another answered, "No, we were just excited. We were afraid. It was dark." The first boy replied, "Oh, God, we must get out of here or we shall lose our minds." Ironically, the boy who was trying to justify their crime, Piggy, went to the fortress to get his glasses from the bully. They had set up a large rock which they could push down on anyone or anything coming up the path. Piggy was stumbling up the path because he could hardly see. He was saying, "Don't you know what is right? Can't you use your minds?" They pushed the rock and dashed Piggy over the cliff and into the ocean.

Finally there was only one rational boy remaining. The mob was hunting him in the jungle. He struggled, exhausted, to the beach and was crawling desperately on the sand. The scene widened to include the outstretched hand of the boy touching the foot of a rescuer who had come to the island. The boys walked dazed onto the beach to the realization of what had happened to them.

Golding has portrayed children in the process of the rapid deterioration of the veneer of rationality and morality which society creates. Throughout the movie ran their chant of celebration: "Kerie Eleison! Kerie Eleison!" The chant which they had learned in their chapels became the pagan cry of their inhuman fury. To teach the words is not enough. We cannot hold our children together by merely going through the motions. Our religious observances and civics courses will not stem the tide of a society molded by conformity, dazed by drugs, and weakened by a chaotic freedom. We are never much more than one generation removed from the savage.

This warning was made clear to me one day as I was riding along listening to the radio. Only half listening, really. Out of the cachophony of sound known as rock music, there came a plaintive refrain: "Save the Children! Save the Country!" It was the rock group, The Fifth Dimension, singing a song the title of which I do not yet know. But I got the message. We had better pay attention to the children!

Phillips Brooks said, "He who helps a child helps humanity with an immediateness which no other help given to human creature can possibly give again." To me, life's greatest symbol of potentiality is a child. Its greatest symbol of waste is a washed-up adult who has thrown his/her life away striving for the wrong goals.

The first thing I want to emphasize is that the potentiality of the child is the responsibility of the adult. You and I are responsible to influence our children toward the highest values in life. This is vividly expressed for me in a poem whose author I do not know:

> I took a piece of plastic clay
> And idly fashioned it one day,
> And as my fingers pressed it still,
> It moved and yielded at my will.
> I came again when days were past.
> The form I gave it still it bore,
> And I could change that form no more.
>
> I took a piece of living clay
> And gently formed it day by day,
> And molded with my power and art
> A young child's soft and yielding heart.
> I came again when days were gone.
> It was a man I looked upon.

He still that early impress bore,
And I could change that form no more.

We must develop the potential of the child while he/
she is still a child. Images are formed primarily in the
home. Role models are developed in the home, the school,
and the church. We simply *must* pay more attention to the
examples we are setting for our children. We *must* be
more alert to the values formed by television programs.
We *must* make sure that our beliefs do not remain mere
unspoken assumptions.

When you show your children what your values are
by the way you live, there is not likely to be anyone who
can convince them otherwise. A child can read your
character before he/she can read the alphabet. Sometimes our children do not live up to our expectations for
them, but there is a high probability that they *will* live up
to an example consistently and early set. If you want your
children to hold onto faith in God, you had better show
some faith yourself. If you want them to be loyal to the
church, your loyalty had better be more than a sometime
thing.

Secondly, I want to emphasize that we are responsible to prevent the poisoning of our children's minds.
We are going to have to be a step ahead of their peers,
and a step ahead of the entertainment media. But after
all, God *has* given you a running start! Television cannot
be used as a baby sitter unless you want to turn your
children's minds over to the cartoon makers.

The polluted moral atmosphere of our time is not
primarily hard-core pornography. It is the easy assumption that our responsibility is only to our own pleasure,
our own desires at a given moment. We *must* create in
our children a vital sense of their own personal worth and
dignity. We *must* enable them to distinguish actions which

will be productive of good in the world. We can only do that from the strong foundation of our personal example.

Finally, I want to return to the beginning and emphasize the fact that a society is judged by what happens to its children. Even more so, a family is judged by what happens to its children. And a *church* is judged by what happens to its children. In Houston, Texas a two year old child was summoned to jury duty. Perhaps that was a suggestive error. The children *are* our jury.

We have become extremely concerned in recent weeks that a child murderer may be stalking the streets of southwest Atlanta. Everything possible must be done to stop that person. But what about the more subtle murders which take place every day? What about the children who are being stifled by inattention? What about those who are too weak to stand against the ravages of peer pressure?

One of the most traumatic experiences of my life occurred when I was a very young pastor in a small town. A man in a drunken stupor walked into a room where his son was sitting. He said, "Son, look up the barrel of this gun." When the son trustingly looked up the barrel of that shotgun, the father blew his head nearly off. I went to the jail to talk with the man. He was inconsolable. His cries could be heard all over town.

As I talked with the man I felt ill. I could hardly stand to be in the room with him. In all honesty I told him that whatever society did to him it was what he deserved. But I was there representing the God who loved him and would forgive him. He began to be more calm. I asked the sheriff to call me if he became upset again. Later that week he talked with his lawyer who told him his chances (which were slim and none). He became upset, but they did not call me until the next morning. They had found him on the floor of his cell with his throat cut. In his despair he had taken his own life.

I was angry that I had not been called, but it was too late. Only God can help in a situation so tragic and volatile as that. I remembered something he had said as he had calmed down a few nights before. He said, "That old gun always did have a hair-trigger." Perhaps he was trying to say that he had not intended for his son to die. I think he could not live with himself after what happened.

That event is not relevant to any immediate concern of yours. But I share it with you because we point more loaded death-weapons into the faces of our children than we are willing to admit. Television is loaded. Automobiles are loaded. Alcohol is loaded. Apathy about God and the Church is loaded. Insensitivity is loaded. I wonder what damage children suffer when parents will not take the time really to *listen* to them? I wonder how many children slowly suffocate spiritually simply because some parents are too unconcerned to take them to Sunday School? I wonder how many children wither on the vine when Sunday School teachers are unprepared and give the impression that they are merely going through the motions?

It is time to be more alert, more responsive, more responsible concerning the children of our society. Yes, the responsibility is yours, even if you do not have any children. I hope this poem will leave us all thinking:
"O God!" I cried. "Why may I not forget?
These boys and girls entering life's battle
throng me yet,
Am I their keeper -- only I -- to bear
This constant burden for their good and care?
So often have I seen them led in paths of sin.
Would that my eyes had never opened been!"
The thorn crowned and patient one replied,
"They thronged me too: I too have seen."

126

"So many others go at will," I said,
    protesting still.
"They go unheeding, but these boys and girls,
Willful and thoughtless, yes, and those that sin,
Drag at my heart. For them I serve and groan.
Why is it? Let me rest Lord. I have tried."
He turned and looked at me, "But I have died."

"But Lord, this ceaseless travail of my soul!
This stress! This often fruitless toil,
these souls to win!
They are not mine."
He turned and looked at them, the look of one
    Divine!
Then turned and looked at me. "But they are
    mine."

"O God," I said. "I understand at last.
Forgive, and henceforth I will bondslave be
To thy least, frailest little one;
I would not more be free."
He smiled and said, "It is to me."
                              (Author unknown)

18

FANTASYLAND

"Do not lay up for yourselves treasures on earth, where moth and rust consume and where thieves break in and steal, but lay up for yourselves treasures in heaven, where neither moth nor rust consumes and where thieves do not break in and steal.   Matthew 6:19-20

Walt Disney has created a financial empire, and millions of happy hours for people, by capitalizing upon children's fantasies. Disneyworld is an entertaining place. The worlds of science fiction, the American frontier and fairy tales come delightfully alive.

We took our children to Disneyworld and spent two wonderful days -- standing in line! We rode the space ship. We toured the frontier village, and we saw Mickey Mouse in person. I tell you, a man has to be a genius to build an empire around a rat! I really enjoyed seeing Mickey and Minnie, Goofy, and the three little pigs. That took me back to my childhood. Nostalgia is a powerful emotion.

When I was growing up, the story of the three little pigs was often made into a spine-tingling episode by an

imaginative parent. Each of the three little pigs set off
to establish his fortune. In each case, the first order of
business was to build a house. The first little pig built
his house of straw. The wicked wolf blew his house down
and ate him! The second little pig built his house of sticks.
Likewise, the wicked wolf blew his house down and ate
him! But the third little pig was more enterprising and
industrious. He built his house of bricks. He was so secure that he finally killed the wolf as he tried to come
down the chimney.

That story reinforced the strongly accentuated vir-
tues of diligence, hard work, and industriousness at that
time. It also focused upon the foremost psychological
need — survival in the face of threat. The human impulse
to survival is overwhelming --and for good reason! Survival gives meaning to life. Jesus was aware of that when
he made his references to "when the wolf comes," and to
"laying up treasures in heaven" rather than on earth.
(John 10:12)

The survival mentality is a mentality of desperation.
It is reflected in monuments to that desperation. The
older ones of you may recall the Maginot Line in France
as a frantic effort to safeguard that nation from the threat
of German attack. The younger ones of you may remember when Americans were building and stocking atom bomb
shelters with food for survival and guns for keeping their
neighbors out. The insurance industry in America thrives
upon our deep need to provide security for our families in
the face of the prospect that we may not survive to care
for them. Which of us does not wish that he could afford
more life insurance or some other form of financial security? The urge to survive is overwhelming!

Equally strong, though not as universal, is the urge
to power and grandeur. When the possibility for power increases, the urge for grandeur takes over. When a

preacher gets in position to become a bishop, a new mo-
tivation becomes operative. If he becomes a bishop, he
begins to consider what history will say of him. Bishop
Arthur Moore was our bishop in Georgia for twenty years.
He wore the mantle of authority with dignity and grace.
The story is told that on one occasion he entered the elevator in a building in Chicago. The elevator operator took
one look at him and said, "Good morning, Governor."
Bishop Moore replied, "I am not a governor." The operator said, "Well, good morning, Senator." Again the
bishop replied, "I am not a Senator. I am a bishop of the
Methodist Church." The elevator operator paused a moment and said, "Well, Bishop, I knew that whatever rac-
ket you were in, you were the head of it!"

Throughout history, power and grandeur have gone
hand in hand. The pyramids of Egypt, the temples of
Solomon and Herod, the Colliseum of Rome, the Parthe-
non of Athens, all stood as triumphs of grandeur. They
were also grandly frantic attempts to survive! They became monuments of futility.

I have seen what is left of Solomon's Temple -- a
few pieces of rubble -- themselves questionable. I have
seen what is left of Herod's Temple -- a piece of a wall!
Massive, yes! But horribly futile. I watched as people
living in their own incapsulated world of anticipation -- an
anticipation not shared by the overwhelming majority of
their countrymen -- stand at the wall of Herod's Temple
and pray fervently for a messiah whom Christians believe
they have already missed, and about whom the rest of the
world does not care. Their messiah was a messiah of
material splendor -- an illusion of grandeur.

The story of the three little pigs is a fairy tale. But
so is every effort to establish a foundation for survival on
the sands of time. Disneyworld is a fantasyland, and is
intended to be so. One is not supposed to live there. I

entered the magnificent looking castle. It was a disappointment. It was only a gift shop and a restaurant. One does not live on trinkets and bread. It is not enough. Every one of us discovers that fact deep inside sooner or later.

Jesus tried to tell us that man does not live by bread alone. He also tried to teach us that the urge to grandeur is an intimation of the Kingdom of God -- not the "magic kingdom." Nothing that we can build will ultimately survive. The only grandeur worthy of the name is the grandeur of the human spirit -- the abundant life which Jesus offered. This is why Jesus did not *build* the Kingdom of God. He *announced* it. He proclaimed it. One does not build the Kingdom of God; he *lives* in it.

What survives is the cup of cold water given in Jesus' name. What survives is the well of living water bursting forth from within the human spirit. What survives is the treasure laid up in heaven where moth and rust do not corrupt and the forces of thievery, greed, and human perversity do not apply.

If you want to build something that will last -- something that is grand -- build *yourself* into the fabric of caring, helping, serving humanity. Build that which flows within the stream of human history, which flows and grows and emerges with time -- not that which is ravaged by time.

Build on the foundation on which no other foundation can be laid -- Jesus Christ. Build his Church. Paul said to those Christians at Corinth who had been caught up in the power and grandeur of the Corinthian charismatic movement: "... since you are so eager for manifestations of the Spirit, strive to excel in building up the Church." (I Corinthians 14:12)

Build a pattern of discipleship. Jesus said, "Every-one who hears these words of mine and does them will be like a wise man who built his house upon a rock; and the rain fell and the floods came and the wind blew and beat upon that house, but it did not fall, because it had been founded on the rock." (Matthew 7:24,25) To be a disciple means to be taught -- and to be teachable. So many times we learn a little *about* Jesus and a little *from* Jesus and then we stop learning. To build a pattern of discipleship means that we determine to learn from Jesus *all our lives*. We remain open to *all* truth insofar as we can per-ceive it. We remain open to all people in the hope that we may continue to learn *from them*.

Build a habit of stewardship. All you have is time or some congealed essence of it. You pay staff salaries be-cause you want the full time of those people. You pay build-ing maintenance because you cannot or do not want to do it yourself. You pay insurance because you want to guard against the massive time requirements of rebuilding in case of disaster. You send mission gifts as an extension of or a substitute for yourself. Your stewardship is the *investment of yourself*. Your money is one form of you. The Lord's Church cannot function in today's world without both aspects of yourself. It was never intended to do so. We should have learned that from the story of Ananias and Sapphira in the book of Acts (Chapter 5). They could have kept their money and their time, but they said, "We want to belong to Christ." Then they proceeded to cheat him by lying about their possessions to the church. Ananias and Sapphira both dropped dead as a result of their lie. They might as well have -- because living a lie is the supreme exercise in futility. That is what John meant when he reported the Holy Spirit's word to the church at Sardis: "I know your works; you have the name of being alive, and you are dead." (Revelation 3:1) Stewardship is the way of life, not of death!

The final suggestion I want to make is this: build a context of churchmanship. Recognize that the development of your life and loyalties through the Church of Jesus Christ is not just stewardship; it is churchmanship. It is the awareness of corporate strength. There are ministries of worship and witness and service that we can only do together. Christ did not merely instruct his disciples and scatter them to the winds of history. He built his Church. He called them *together* as a force against which the gates of hell shall not prevail! *That* is the grandeur of the Kingdom of God -- its proclamation, its service, its intimation for the future -- and we are a part of it!

19

THE SHADOW OF THE CROSS

It was now about the sixth hour, and there
was darkness over the whole land....
                                           Luke 23:44

It may seem incongruous to you that we are reading
and talking about the cross of Jesus the week after Easter.
This is supposed to be a glorious time, a victorious time
in which all earthly problems have been surmounted -- at
least in principle, awaiting the "second coming" of our
Lord. That is the easy way out. As a matter of fact, reflection about the cross really intensified after the resurrection. What does the cross of Jesus *mean* for the world?
Friedrich Nietzsche observed that the idea of a God on a
cross reversed all the values of antiquity. That is correct,
and the reverberations of the cross are striking us now
more forcefully than ever.

...At twelve noon on the day we call "Good Friday,"
when Jesus of Nazareth hung on the cross, no one seemed
to notice the faintly dim spot on the earth beneath him. It
was a natural thing -- just the shadow of his cross. But by

three in the afternoon, when the sun had brightened and the angle of sun and cross were more extended, the shadow of the cross stretched its accusing finger over all Jerusalem.

That haunting finger pointed inexorably toward those closed-minded religious leaders who considered any different idea as a threat to God himself. The dark finger accused, as if to reaffirm that personal goodness is not enough. Conscience, no matter how alert, can fall victim to the most grievous errors in the name of righteousness.

The accusing finger of God cast its judgment upon those leaders of the business community, the Sadducees. They were the people who had to be dealt with if any move of any kind were to be successful in Israel. The Sadducees included a combination of priestly and civil power available to deal with the Romans -- or whatever government happened to gain control in Palestine. Their primary question was: "Is it good for business?" There seems to be little doubt that Jesus became a man marked for extermination the day he interfered in the economic affairs of the Temple.

The accusing finger of God reached all the way to the isolated spot where the lifeless body of Judas hanged. How strange it is that we rarely seem to assume that the dictum: "It were better for that man if he had never been born" could apply to any one of us! Yet judgment has always been the more harsh upon those who have been known as friends of God -- but who have turned their backs on him when their interests and priorities were transformed by the alchemy of greed.

By late afternoon the dark shadow of the cross spread its accusing presence over all Jerusalem -- that unlikely combination of political and military power and the indeterminate "people." Let us mark it well, Pontius Pilate was conscious of the "people" when he made his infamous judgment. From that day to this, legal and political judgments have been made with a sensitive eye to what the "people" would tolerate.

Now, for two thousand years the sun has been sinking toward the horizon of human history. The shadow of the cross is so long that it covers the whole world and the span of human concerns. The same forces are at work: religious bigotry, business and power-vested manipulations of social forces (without regard for moral considerations), political expediency and military efficiency.

It is our time and place, and the issues have never been more sharply focused. The cross of Jesus stands as a giant exclamation point on the horizon of our consciousness! Do you see it? The exclamation point is at the end of this sentence: "Blessed are you poor, for yours is the Kingdom of God!" (Luke 6:20)

The judgment of the cross includes all the forces we have mentioned, but the issue today is the poor. What does God want us to do about the poor? We are threatened in this country with the prospect that the poor could become relatively invisible again. There is a discernible tendency in our national life to ignore, even deny, the existence of the poor. We now have in the White House, in the role of chief adviser to the President on the domestic economy, one Martin Anderson, who recently wrote a book "proving" that there are no poor people in the United States! With this kind of mentality at the center of our national life, the shadow of the cross will be dark, indeed!

As the trickles of information and misinformation come in from Latin America, we are going to find ourselves increasingly disconcerted and confused with the flow of events. That great monolith of conservatism, the Roman Catholic Church, is now being accused of being subversive!

It is only about a year since Archbishop Oscar Romero was assassinated in El Salvador while celebrating mass. Why did this soft-spoken pastor, who had always concentrated on the spiritual life, move to becoming an outspoken opponent of the military repression and political violence in his country? The more recent slaughter of four women missionaries caught our attention. But we may have failed to notice the 14,000 deaths of persons in that country at the hands of political terrorists on both sides. (The word "terrorist" is usually reserved for the non-governmental atrocity-mongers. Government atrocity is called "security!")

We might as well face it now, the more the Church comes under the shadow of the cross, the more it will identify with the poor and the oppressed -- and the more suspect it will be in the eyes of those who are obsessed with the arrogance of power and the insensitivity of vested interests. If you advocate human rights, *and mean it,* you will become the enemy of those who disregard those rights.

We may wonder what we have to do with El Salvador. El Salvador is at the doorstep of the United States, and the battle for the poor is already in process right here. That is why, slowly but surely, you will see the Church divided as people choose sides, and the shadow of the cross becomes more apparent over our national life.

Our hope lies in the fact that the shadow of the cross is not merely an accusing finger. It is an outstretched hand -- an open hand, an inviting hand. Jesus said, "Come unto me all you who labor and are heavy laden..."

It has been suggested that moralisms are irrelevant in the face of the social forces and economic issues which will determine the destiny of our times. Perhaps so, but the cross of Jesus Christ is not a moralism. It is a power of the love of almighty God. We are committed to the belief that the power of God will make a difference in this world.

The shadow of the cross is not primarily an indict-ment. It is an invitation. The shadow is not created by the cross alone. It is created by the correlation of the cross to the light which transcends it.

Christ takes us beyond the sinfulness of human beings to the light of God's forgiving purpose. The dark deeds of our human experience are enough to make any perceptive person despair. Yet the light of God's pro-mise keeps on shining. In spite of everything, God is reaching out his reconciling arms of love to us. You and I are instruments of his love.

That is everything.

138

20

THE CREATIVE SPIRIT

*In the beginning God created the heavens
and the earth. The earth was without form and
void, and darkness was upon the face of the deep;
and the Spirit of God was moving over the face of
the waters.*

Genesis 1:1,2

Have you ever thought about the fact that there was
a time when everything we have did not exist? There was
a time when there was no such thing as a computer, or a
telephone, an automobile, an airplane, or an atom bomb.

There was a time when there was no such thing as a
door, a spoon, or a wheel. From the simplest tool to the
most complex instrument, everything was made by someone. But before it was made it was a *thought* in someone's
mind -- or a problem, a question, a possibility.

The combination of thought and energy produced the
toothpick, the knife, the spear. A similar combination of
thought and energy developed the crystal radio, the vacuum
tube, and the transistor. Everything we possess had an
inventor. Most of what we now have has been developed

over a period of time. One could say that these things
evolved as persons adapted their instruments to their
needs.

How is it that we can understand human creativity
but seem to be unable to grasp the idea that the world is
the result of the correlation of thought and energy?

Just as there seems to be something in the relation
of persons to objects which makes *creativity* possible,
there also seems to be something in the relation of persons to persons which makes *society* possible. We can
see the difference between the cell division of simple animal life and the complexity of human social activity.

What is it that makes social life possible? For want
of a better word we call this *spirit*, or mind. Human
beings relate to each other by body and mind. The physical relationship is enhanced by an additional aspect. It is
not sufficient merely to be *alive*. The *relation* is what
offers (socially and biologically) creative possibility.

When the Bible speaks of the beginning of this world,
it is describing a *relation*. "And the Spirit of God was
moving over the face of the waters."

"Wait a minute, preacher! You are moving too fast!
What is this Spirit of God?"

"Sorry!"

In the last few thousand years we have come to what
we think is a fair understanding of this combination of
thought and energy which makes the world possible. Again,
for want of a better word, we call this God. (He or she
or it has been called by many names.) God makes *creativity* possible. Spirit is that aspect or characteristic of
human life which pertains to our relationships. The Spirit

of God is *God*, creating by his thought and energy a relationship between himself and the world. The relationship
is consummated between God and human beings.

The author of the creation account was describing
the relation of the world to its origin in thought and energy.
It was a *personal* relationship. More than that, the author
was describing the relationship which was the focal point
of his society. That relationship was between Spirit and
spirit -- of ultimate infinite Spirit with human finite spirit.
His language was: "And the Spirit of God was moving..."

We may or may not deny the relationship, but the
problem is not the language. As long as the relationship
is viable the language is useful. We need not expect the
scientific or the secular community to use this language.
But we in the Church can and should use it.

"And the Spirit of God was moving...."

ABRAHAM sensed the presence of God and came to
understand the nature of the relationship. "I will be your
God and you will be my people," said the Lord. There
was a reciprocal aspect to the relationship which we call
"covenant." The covenant required faithfulness -- each to
the other.

The Spirit of God was with JOSEPH as he was sold
into slavery in Egypt. Joseph was given the courage to
remain morally true to God in the face of temptation. He
was given the gift of profound insight into the meaning of
dreams. He was given wisdom to rule Egypt.

The Spirit of God was with MOSES as he spoke the
word of the Lord to Pharoah, "Let my people go." God
was leading the children of Israel (Jacob) out of bondage
in Egypt. God was with the Israelites in the desert of Sinai
as they pondered their response to the God who had been

faithful in delivering them from bondage. The development of Hebrew (Israelite) ethics was an elaboration of
the meaning of that reciprocal question: what does it mean
to be faithful to the God who has been faithful to us?

The Spirit of God was with SAUL as he was anointed
to be King of Israel. He was with DAVID as he led Israel
to greatness and worldly glory. God gave SOLOMON
great wisdom as he expanded and established the kingdom.

The Spirit of God was with the HEBREW PROPHETS
as they discerned the will of God. God gave them courage
and insight as he called his people to repentance and faithfulness. God was with his people in their accomplishments and their discouragements, in their destructions
and their rebuilding, in their exiles and their returns
from exile.

The psalm writers expressed a keen awareness of
the presence of God in their lives and in the life of the
community of Israel. God reminded them of their need
for him. He cleansed them of their guilt. He strengthened
them in the face of enormous difficulties. The agony and
the ecstasy of Israel is reflected in their psalms. The
Spirit of God was with them every moment and in every
situation. Typical are these expressions from the 139th
Psalm:
O Lord, thou has searched me and known me!
Thou knowest when I sit down and when I rise up;
Thou discernest my thoughts from afar.
--- Thou searchest out my path and my lying down,
and art acquainted with all my ways. . . .

Whither shall I go from thy Spirit?
Or whither shall I flee from thy presence?
If I ascend into heaven, thou art there!
If I make my bed in Sheol, thou art there!
If I take the wings of the morning

and dwell in the uttermost parts of the sea,
even there thy hand shall lead me,
and thy right hand shall hold me....

Thou didst form my inward parts,
Thou didst knit me together
in my mother's womb....

How precious to me are thy thoughts, O God!
How vast is the sum of them!
If I would count them,
they are more than the sand.
When I awake, I am still with thee....

Search me, O God, and know my heart!
Try me and know my thoughts!
And see if there be any wicked way in me,
and lead me in the way everlasting!

The Spirit of God was with the MACCABEES as they threw off the yoke of foreign oppression. He was with the PHARISEES as they tried diligently to translate obedience into a daily program of activity.

Until the time of the coming of the Christ we can see this golden thread of God's presence holding the Hebrew community in covenant. That thread points like an arrow toward the ultimate presence of God in Jesus, the Christ.

The Spirit of God was with MARY as she bore the infant Jesus. He anointed JESUS with the presence of the heavenly dove. God's presence and power are seen as inseparable from Jesus himself, so much so that John could proclaim:

For the law was given through Moses; grace and
truth came through Jesus Christ. No one has
ever seen God; the only Son, who is in the bosom
of the Father, he has made him known. (1:17, 18)

The power of Christ to heal and the will of Christ to reveal are both expressions of the oneness of Jesus with the Spirit of God. This oneness is continued at Pentecost in the giving of the Spirit to the Church. The gifts of the Spirit *to* the Church and the fruit of the Spirit *in* the Church are equally expressions of God's creative and renewing activity in the world.

The two thousand year history of the Church is a testimony to the continuation of the creative and renewing activity of God. Every sin which characterized the Hebrew people has been duplicated by Christians. Yet the Spirit of God continues to call *both* covenant peoples to repentance and faithfulness. Every day is an expression of the "Spirit of God moving...."

The Spirit of God is moving in Decatur First United Methodist Church. The future of this church is God's creative opportunity. The celebration of Pentecost is coming around again. Always, as God's people have celebrated their history, it was an occasion for the expression of God's renewing presence.

One of the most exciting events I know anything about in a church is our Pentecost Arts Festival. Not that it will be good -- we know it will be good! Everything you do here is well planned and well carried out. The important thing to realize is that it is an opportunity to be reminded of the breadth and variety of the gifts and capacities which God gives to us.

Further, the festival gets away from some of the more traditional ways of thinking about God's activity. We may discover more and more different avenues of his working among us.

What will God do for you? What gifts has he given

you? What fruits of the Spirit will you express: love, joy, peace, patience, what?

Perhaps no one has explained to you the logo of our church. You have seen it prominantly displayed for more than a year. The logo consists of a small case "d" over which rests a hovering dove. Of course, the "d" represents Decatur and the dove represents the Spirit of God. The Spirit is hovering -- waiting to bless us, to strengthen us, to express himself through us. But he is waiting for *us to respond to him!* After all, response is what a *relationship* is all about! How will you respond?

21

CARRYING THE FIRE

"I came to cast fire on the earth; and
would that it were already kindled."
                                    Luke 12:49

One of the more thrilling events of the Olympic Games
occurs when the runner brings the flame from Mount Olym-
pus for the beginning of the games. From the time of the
original games in Greece to the present, this act has symbolized the spirit of competition. As the Olympic Games
are the highest form of competition in human racing, so
for me the Indianapolis 500 is the zenith of automobile racing. During the entire race spectators experience the
highest automobile driving performance where disaster
lurks as each driver's constant companion.

In this year's race Danny Ongais' car struck the wall
and disintegrated in an instant. A great ball of fire went
up from the car and firemen rushed to extinguish the flames.
I could see Ongais' body slumped in the skeletal wreckage of
the car -- his feet and legs hanging ominously over the
front framework. Miraculously, he survived.

At about the same time, Johnny Mears' car came into the pits and the crew hurried to douse his car with the fire extinguishers. The announcers explained that it was an alcohol fire, and an alcohol fire is invisible. I could see some of the crewmen dancing wildly, throwing their arms in all directions. They were calling for aid, because they were on fire too! To be on fire is a frightening experience!

Fire symbolizes and embodies the most awesome and awful experiences of human life. The blaze can be warm and comforting -- or it can be raging and utterly destructive.

Anyone who has been in war knows the horror which fire can create. In the Viet Nam War we honed the horror of fire to a fine edge with napalm. Anyone who has experienced a power failure in mid-winter has at least some indication of what discomfort a lack of fire would entail.

In the Old Testament, fire symbolized the violent judgment of God. The first actual reference is in the nineteenth chapter of Genesis, and says: "Fire from the Lord out of heaven" destroyed the cities of the plain. Fire also symbolized the cleansing and purifying presence of God -- the testing of faith and character of an individual or of God's people.

Pre-modern man expressed a *mythological* understanding of the significance of fire. Fire was seen by the Greeks as the civilizer of humankind. Fire was the prerogative of the gods. After all, lightning was probably the earliest source of fire, and even fire by friction had its mysterious aspect. The Greeks explained the possession of fire with the myth of Prometheus.

Prometheus, in a glorious act of defiance of the gods, steals fire from Zeus and brings it to earth in a hollow stalk. For this, Prometheus was punished by being bound to a stake. His liver was daily, and endlessly, consumed by a vulture. Thus, human misery and glory are associated in Greek mythology with fire and defiance of the gods.

The power of the myth of Prometheus continues into our own time as an expression of modern man's psychological situation: guilty, rebellious, frustrated, unsure of himself, alienated, yet seeking to assert himself. Man's finitude is seen as an heroic struggle against death. Such a point of view can only end in some form of resolute despair. This despair takes many forms -- from the bravado of the existentialist philosopher who insists that he must give his life its own ultimate meaning, to the inveterate "goer and doer" who seems condemned to live out his life in the hope of some impossible ecstasy.

Modern man expresses his understanding of the significance of fire in a *technological* sense. Fire is energy. As such, it portends either a materialistic utopia or an ultimate holocaust. Most of us can hardly comprehand the horrible implications of a cobalt bomb firestorm. Nevertheless, we live with it -- perched precariously on the edge of our consciousness.

More tolerable to contemplate, while still dangerous, are the other technological uses of fire. Michael Collins describes his experiences as an astronaut and his journey to the moon. He says: "'Carrying the fire' is simply what I feel space flight is like, when limited to three words."

It is not too difficult to imagine the astronauts sitting in their spacecraft atop a flaming Saturn rocket as it lifts off from earth. They hold with quiet desperation to the ejection ring between their knees during those first totally precarious seconds. As Collins says, "How do you carry fire? Very carefully, that's how, with lots of planning and considerable risk."

This is where we are today -- modern man the fire
carrier -- energy conscious, faced with immense technological possibilities, yet threatened. We *are* on space
ship Earth -- and there is an alarmingly large number
of hands on the ejection rings. There are those who are
dedicated to carrying the fire "very carefully... with lots
of planning (amidst) considerable risk." We can be thankful and gain a measure of momentary security in that
thought.

Nevertheless, I am convinced that an additional understanding is essential -- a *theological* one. More precisely, a *Christian* theological one. As long as man the
fire carrier understands himself in a Promethean sense,
his fire is an act of defiance and his life is an endurance
of inevitable pain, either physical or psychological -- or
both. The result of this is a certain sense of inevitability
-- that man will destroy himself; that suffering is somehow understandable (and appropriate.)

When we understand man the fire carrier in a theological sense, we begin to come to grips with John's pro-
nouncement:
>"I baptize you with water; but he who is
>mightier than I is coming, the thong of
>whose sandals I am not worthy to untie;
>he will baptize you with the Holy Spirit
>and with fire." (Luke 3:16)

And with Jesus' even more mysterious saying:
>"I came to cast fire upon the earth."
>   (Luke 12:49)

The context of Jesus' saying indicates the totality of
his claim and the divisions inherent in conflicting loyalties.
Yet the reference of John the Baptist to the Holy Spirit and
the subsequent references in Acts to the events of Pentecost provide an additional understanding.

> And there appeared to them tongues as of
> fire, distributed and resting on each one
> of them. And they were all filled with the
> Holy Spirit... (Acts 2:3, 4a)

Jesus is the transition point in which fire is not ultimately judgment, nor even cleansing -- but power! The power does not need to be stolen, in some sort of primordial act of defiance. One need not find himself in self-assertion -- however bold -- but in self-acceptance in which one's selfhood is understood as a gift from God.

Man does not achieve his salvation by stealing fire from heaven, but by receiving it as a gift. The Holy Spirit comes to cleanse our minds, rejuvenate our motives, and equip us for abundant living. Living with guilt is neither inevitable nor desirable. There is no need to be eternally bound, with the vulture of our finitude picking away daily at our liver.

Thomas Merton makes a highly illuminating comment on this point:

> Not knowing that the fire was his for the
> asking, not knowing that fire was something
> that God created expressly for man,
> Prometheus felt he had to steal it. But
> why? Because he knew no god that would
> be willing to give it to him for nothing.
> He knew no god that was not an enemy,
> because the only gods he knew were only
> a little stronger than himself. He had to
> steal the fire from the gods that were
> weak. If he had known the strong God,
> everything would have been quite different.

We no longer have to steal the fire! Christ has given it to us! In Christ we experience, not the purging of fire, but the purity of forgiveness. In the Holy Spirit we are given power for living and strength for service. Thus, we become fire carriers, carrying within us the fire of God's presence and power. How do you carry fire? "Very carefully, with lots of planning and considerable risk."

This is why it is so necessary for anyone who has experienced the power and presence of the Holy Spirit to be warned against the Promethean tendency to use it for himself -- to seek the glory of the Holy Spirit for one's own satisfaction. Thus, one steals the fire, instead of allowing the fire to be an instrument of God within oneself.

This is why Elton Trueblood insists that the only way to be loyal to the fire of Christ is to spread it. This is why Emil Brunner can say, "The church exists by mission as fire exists by burning." The Holy Spirit gives us purpose and power. We are the fire carriers. How is the spark in us? Do we have enough to share? If we have any at all, we *must* share!